# Into the Dawn

## A Memoir of Eric Badke

Into the Dawn
Copyright © 2017
ISBN : 978-1543249453

All rights reserved. No part of this book may be reproduced in any form without written permission from Eric Badke
eric-badke@live.ca

Cover design by David Burton

Book description by Gerald Bouwknecht

All scripture is taken from the New king James Version. Copyright © 1982 by Thomas Nelson, Inc. Used by permission. All rights reserved.

**Eric Badke**

> The way of the righteous
> is like the first gleam of dawn,
> which shines ever brighter
> until the full light of day.
> Proverbs 4:18

# Chapter 1

...When my case was called and the prosecutor read the charges, the detail of my crimes, I kept my composure. After my attorney spoke in my defense it was time for the judge to go into his chambers to review my case.

After the judge deliberated and came back into the courtroom the bailiff yelled out,

"All rise!"

When the judge sat down we followed suit. He peered at me over his glasses and told me to rise.

"Eric Badke, after much consideration and due to the seriousness of your crimes, I sentence you to twelve months open custody!" He then slammed down the gavel and departed.

I was extremely shocked. What did this mean? I was shaking my head trying to process the ruling the judge meted out. I was undeniably not going home for lunch on that ill-fated day.

The sheriff came over to me, grabbed my arm and led me out of the courtroom. He brought me to the back of courthouse to where the cells were and proceeded to lock me in. I sat there on a hard bench for three hours in confusion, still trying to comprehend what had just happened to me.

The year was 1989, I was seventeen, and I was going to be in prison for a whole year! That is a long time!

**Eric Badke**

What led me to this level of degradation and degeneration? How could I have sunk so low? I began reflecting about my childhood and how my life began.

My parents met in Summerland, British Columbia in 1971. Summerland is a small town in the Okanagan valley between Kelowna and Penticton. They encountered each other at a hippie peace gathering in which there were countless individuals walking hand in hand down the street singing various peace songs. My mom joined hands with my dad for the first time and their attraction to each other was the beginning of a meaningful relationship.

My dad's name is Gary and he is of German descent and my mom's name is Beverly and she is of Okanagan/Salish First Nations decent. When they met, my mom was sixteen and my dad was nineteen.

My dad, who lived in Kelowna at the time, would often make the one hour drive from Kelowna to Penticton to visit my mom on the native reservation. My dad became somewhat famous on the reservation because he resembled General Custer, who died in the American Indian wars in 1876. Dad even wore a hat like Custer which made it even more comical. So from then on he was known affectionately as General Custer on the reserve, and everyone liked and accepted him.

Not long afterwards my parents got married and moved into a house in Kelowna. In October 1971 my mom conceived and in 1972, July the 24th, I came forth into the world.

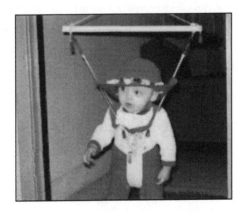

**Eric at age one**

Job 3:11 in the Bible says, *"Why did I not die at birth? Why did I not perish when I came from the womb?"*

There were many times later in life when I would ask the same questions Job asked in his torment. I was born with asthma and atopic dermatitis (eczema) which added to the misery during my years of difficulty. In truth, the reality was that God had shone a light on the day I was born even though I wouldn't realize it until decades later.

**Eric Badke**

One year and four days after I was born, 1973, the 28th day of July, mom gave birth to my younger brother Roland. He was a gift from God and would become my companion throughout all life's struggles and difficulties. He would always be that one constant throughout my life, for which I am eternally grateful.

Life was a challenge for me right from the beginning. My first memory was from when I was two years old. It took place one summer evening when we had a gathering from my mom's side of the family at our house. They had just come from a funeral and were mourning one of my young cousins who was run over by a car and killed a week previous. Since they were drinking and getting fairly rowdy, I was getting nervous. I soon realized I was alone with these strangers and desperately needed the security of my dad. I asked someone where he was and they replied, "He went to the store with your uncle Rob."

Immediately I panicked and desperately wanted to be with my dad so I proceeded to run out the front door. I still remember my tiny bare feet slapping against the sidewalk pavement as I ran towards the carport where my dad and uncle were warming up the car. Just as I ran behind the car my dad backed up and ran me over!

Suddenly I found myself in the front seat of the car between my dad and my uncle. I was relieved and delighted.

As the car pulled out the headlights lit up on a little boy who was curled up on the driveway. I remember wondering who that little boy was and perhaps I could play with him later. For some reason my dad and my uncle panicked and yelled out in distress. I noticed my uncle fumbling at the door handle trying to get out. What I didn't know at the time was that little boy on the driveway was me and I was having an out-of-body experience. I was in the second realm, or as others call it: the spirit world.

The next thing I remembered was that I was lying on a bed in the hospital. My dad was in the room along with doctors and nurses who were attending to me. I left my body again and floated upwards toward the ceiling where I could watch the events that were happening in the room below me. I observed my dad's eyes roll back as he fell backwards onto the floor. The trauma of the situation made him pass out I later recollected but at the time I was confused about what was happening. A nurse was now attending to him as well. This was all so very strange to me.

A few moments later another nurse came into the room. There was something different about this nurse. She was gazing at me with a kindhearted expression on her face. She reached her hand up and I took it. I floated like a balloon as she pulled me towards her. As I stood beside her there was something tranquil about her that kept me calm.

She led me out into the hallway of the hospital and pointed to a wooden barred crib that was hanging from the hallway ceiling by a thick chain. Without saying a word, as she didn't need to, she carried me up a wooden stepladder, placed me in the crib, and departed. I remember feeling nothing but peace, safety, and composure in that crib as I watched people walking to and fro down the hallway below me.

Unexpectedly my mom and uncle appeared at the end of the hallway and began walking towards me. Immediately I became thrilled to see my mom and uncle! I continued to call out to them until they were right below me. They both looked very anxious and upset. My exhilaration soon turned into frustration as my mom seemingly ignored me and walked into the room that I had just come out of. She wasn't ignoring me she just couldn't hear or see me!

That is all I can remember from that event.

My dad told me later on in life that when we got home from the hospital he told our guests that he had run me over with his car earlier. They didn't respond to what he said favorably. They thought he was playing a tasteless joke on them. They were mourning because they had just buried an unfortunate loved one after he was recently run over as I was. They were very upset with my dad and it almost came to blows until my mom and uncle confirmed the truth in what he was telling them.

Thank God the tires of the car didn't roll over my body when my dad ran me over. There would have been two funerals that month!

It wasn't until I was older that I understood what had happened to me and obtained the understanding. Most people do not believe that there is a spirit world but I was there! It wasn't a dream! Even though it was hazy I could see and hear everything that was happening around me while out of the body and in the second realm. I concluded later that the nurse who was looking after me was an angel sent by God in order to keep me safe. When she placed me in that crib God and His angels were watching but they weren't the only ones who were watching. The demonic also took notice that it was God's priority to keep me safe. When they saw that I was valuable to God that meant that one day I could possibly become a threat to them. I had a destiny that they needed to destroy.

A short time later, perhaps a couple of weeks after I was run over, I was soundly asleep in my bed. I abruptly became conscious when an evil demonic entity grabbed my legs and pulled me right out of my body! I was instantaneously aware that I was in danger and was absolutely terrified! I could sense the evil emanating from this dark devil and it was frightening! It proceeded to pull me down the hallway. The level of terror I felt was severe and beyond description. As it pulled me I was weightless and had nothing to grab onto as I was at the mercy of this malevolent being.

It tugged me towards the lit up kitchen where I could see my dad frying up some vegetables on the stove. He was unaware of what was happening to me. I shouted out to my dad and kicked myself free from the grasp this demon had on me. I was frantic as I rapidly glided around my dad. I shrieked out for help and as I coasted around dad I noticed that there were tracers of my body emanating all around him! He could not hear me and to my frustration and distress he just continued what he was doing oblivious to what was taking place. The level of bleakness and futility of my circumstance began to match the dread and trepidation I was experiencing.

Much to my dismay this demonic fiend reinitiated its grasp onto my legs to wrench me away from my dad and advance me towards the stairs that led below towards the ground floor. As it hauled me down the stairs into the dark basement the panic I felt within me was beyond measure! Once down below it proceeded to pull me across the basement toward the adjacent cement wall. Where was it trying to take me? To a place that no person desires to go I'm sure! My demonic adversary went through the wall but although he tried, he couldn't pull me through.

God was now in control as all fear began to depart from my senses. I stayed a moment stuck against the wall. The basement was no longer dark and menacing but set alight and serene. Finally I slid down the wall and began walking across toward the stairs to go back up. As I proceeded, halfway across the basement I began to hear my heart amplified and beating loudly in my ears. Suddenly I was back in my body upstairs in my bed. I felt at ease as if nothing happened. I drifted off into a peaceful sleep.

From that time on I would periodically have unwanted evil experiences as I slept. These nightmarish terrors would have me running all over the house trying to escape them. It is hard if not impossible to explain what was contained within my dreams (if you could call them dreams) but I could say this: They were unnatural, terrifying and evil. I was too young to handle such an onslaught and even as an adult it would have been appallingly intolerable.

Part of me would be aware of my surroundings in the physical but I would be in the spiritual realm as well, being victimized by an exceedingly evil domain. I would wake up my dad and would plead with him to rescue me but there was nothing he could do. Most of the time my panic-stricken episode would have to complete its course until it was finally over. Once it was over my dad and I could finally go back to bed and receive some much needed rest.

If I were to try and explain these experiences, which is almost impossible, I would tell you that many times I would be floating and spinning in a dark abyss. I would feel intense pulsating evil all around me at different frequencies. If I could value the evil at a percentage rate it would begin at 10 per cent and it would gradually rise to 100 per cent, and then it would subside back to 10 per cent; to begin the process again! As the strength of this tangible evil would increase so would the level of my dread. I would almost go out of my mind with panic!

As I was curled up, spinning and floating in this bottomless gulf, along with a shocking fright I would feel a furious anger within me that wasn't my own. My face would glow red and hot from it and I would gnash my teeth together. This is not a place I would wish anyone to go.

I kept having these experiences, but by the time I reached my 20's they evolved into something else entirely.

**Eric Badke**

As an adult, on any given night, I would be asleep in my bed and I would suddenly sense a malicious presence come into my dwelling. I could always sense the location of it in the house. As this phantom would approach my bedroom the level of its malevolence and the alarming terror within me would increase exponentially. This dark spirit would enter my room and I would be paralyzed as it climbed on top of me. As it sat on my chest and ravaged me I couldn't move or cry out a single word! I was completely dominated and at the mercy of this demon as it would propel and deliver its tangible wickedness and fearful horror into my heart and mind! I felt unaided and powerless to fend it off. It had me completely at its mercy, of which it had none.

One night, when I was 28 years old, I was minding my own business sleeping in my bed when this unnatural spiritual intruder came into my house again. As I sensed it getting closer and closer to my room, instead of feeling fear, I felt anger and defiance towards this low spirit. As it was coming down the hall I was once again being weighted down with paralyses.

"Not this time!" I shouted in my mind and I pressed upwards towards the force that was pinning me down.

All of a sudden I felt a release and I sat up quickly, but I wasn't in my bedroom. I sat up into the second realm where it was dark. The next thing I knew I was having an experience beyond all experiences! One of God's celestial angels walked into the room and he was emitting a luminous light and beaming! Light swirled all around him and he was even clothed and cocooned within this magnificent incandescence! This angel that seemingly just dropped in from a heavenly country was beautiful, tall, and connected to God's omnipotent power. He stood and presented himself to me and smiled an affectionate smile like I have never seen before anywhere on this planet! It was otherworldly and adoring! He then spoke to me from his mind, "Eric, you have nothing to worry about."

I was enthralled by this angelic being so I stood up and moved towards him to get a better look. God's power was pulsating from this warrior angel. I could hear it, feel it, and it was almost a mistake to get that close to him. This power, that was probably enough to generate a city, began to terrify me in a different way! A moment later, before his dominating energy became too overwhelming, I snapped out of the experience and I abruptly found myself back within the reality of my bedroom.

I have never had a night terror or been afraid of anything since. Satan was finally stripped of his power to torment me in this way. It would be another three years before I would officially enter the Kingdom of God as one of His converts, but I will write about that later.

**Eric Badke**

## Chapter 2

When I was three years old and my brother was two my parents divorced. I don't remember specific reasons for their divorce but I did hear stories about them having arguments. Dishes and pans were tossed by my mom towards my dad quite frequently. When they split my brother and I went with our mom and we ended up staying at an American Indian Movement (AIM) compound in Penticton. We mainly stayed in our mom's car at night. I don't remember much about this time period but later on in life my mom told me that the three of us had a lot of fun together.

One thing I do recollect was one summer afternoon when a large group of us were having a picnic in one of the many apple orchards that were in the area. After we ate, a bunch of us kids ran out among the trees to play tag. About ten minutes into our game I noticed a large grey item hanging from a lower branch of one of the trees. I liked the shape of it for some reason. I pointed it out to the older kids and they told me to stay away from it. I wasn't about to listen to them. As my curiosity overwhelmed me I walked up to this interesting item and plucked it off the branch.

All of a sudden it felt like my head was on fire and the agony had me screaming! That interesting item I plucked from the tree was a beehive! I couldn't escape the stinging for the life of me. I ran towards the picnic area where my mom was relaxing sitting on a blanket with the other adults. They were confused and wondering why I was running towards them shrieking.

They soon got their answer as they all began to get stung as well. Panic ensued as we all ran to the vehicles to escape the swarm. Unfortunately I got the worst of it as I was stung by over fifty bees!

After this incident I was brought to the Kelowna General hospital where the doctors could examine me. I had an adverse reaction to the bee stings and wasn't in a very good condition at that time. My dad and my grandparents (my dad's parents) were contacted and informed about what had happened. They came to the hospital, observed my condition, and determined that my mom was unfit to have custody of my brother and me. It didn't help my mother's cause that the three of us didn't have an address and we lived in her car.

Social services were contacted by the hospital and they decided to place us in our dad's custody. From then on we lived with our dad, who at the time was living with our grandparents. Life for us became more stable as we dwelled with our dad but we missed our mom terribly. Later on she did come to the house to try to get us back but she was sent away in tears.

My dad has a religion and it is called the Baha'i Faith. This religion teaches that all religions are connected and under one God who sent different prophets to bring a unique message for the time period in which they existed.

Our grandparents were Christians and they believed that there is only one Messiah, one Mediator between God and man - the Savior, Jesus Christ. Only by faith in His sacrifice on the cross for our sins and resurrection from the grave for our justification, can we have a restored relationship with God, an abundant life here on earth and eternal life with Him after we die.

Sometimes when our grandma would tuck us in at bedtime she would talk to Roland and me about Jesus. She would tell us that if we wanted, Jesus would come and live in our hearts. At the time I didn't completely understand what was being offered. How could a man come into our hearts unless he was very small? I visualized a tiny man sitting on a chair in my heart. The idea of that didn't quite appeal to me at that time so I didn't ask Him in.

**Age four & three      Eric's grandparents**

In the 70's it was safe and normal for kids to go out by themselves to explore, so the day after we moved into our grandparents home that is what we did. Our grandparents lived at the base of a small mountain that had a path we could hike along. They also lived in a subdivision full of kids our age that we could play with. The first time Roland and I encountered racism was the first day we went out to play.

We approached a group of kids and one of the older girls told us that we were dirty Indians and that we were bad. I was completely confused because I didn't see that we were any different than them. I didn't know why she was being cruel to us because all we wanted was to be friends and play with them.

Out of the blue a couple of young brothers who lived in the house next to ours came rolling down their driveway in a four-seated go-kart with small inflated, knobby tires. Their dad, who was a mechanic, had put the kart together for them.

They asked us if we wanted to hop on so we did. It was exciting and quite a smooth ride as we coasted along the incline of the road. They introduced themselves as Shawn and Troy. They would become our friends and playmates for most of our childhood. They would join us to go to the beach at Okanagan Lake when grandma took us, and the four of us would hike up the mountain together and enjoy the scenery from one of the cliffs above.

It was on the mountain that I learned about death. I found a robin that wasn't moving. I picked it up and brought it to Shawn and Troy and they told me that it was dead. They mentioned that the same thing would happen to me one day and that idea frightened me. Later on I asked my dad if I was going to die and he replied "Yep" and that settled that. It's amusing to think about now that I look back on it.

When I was five years old our dad decided that he wanted to become a primary school teacher so he left Roland and I in our grandparents care and moved to

Vancouver to attend university. Even though we missed our dad life was exciting being a kid in the 70s.

Our grandpa would periodically take us boat fishing for trout at Beaver Lake, one of the many lakes in the area. It was a great experience, especially when we got a tasty one on the line to bring home for our grandma to fry up.

On some Saturday afternoons we would go to the city dump with grandpa. It was fun going to the dump because Roland and I would explore in the garbage to look for treasures. It was because of the dump that I got into music, as I found a bunch of eight-track tapes during one of my hunts. I brought them home and would play the music on my grandparent's stereo and I enjoyed it. I couldn't believe that someone would throw those out. One man's garbage is another kid's treasure I suppose.

Because our grandparents both worked they would drop us off at Cameron Park Daycare Center every day. We had fun as we made a lot of new friends. We kept ourselves entertained since there was a playground and a wooded area nearby where we could play hide and seek.

After a couple of years we left the daycare and began going to school. I won't go into detail about my time attending school but I do have a few amusing stories to tell.

I am going to tell you about the first time I attempted to steal. I was six years old and attending grade one at North Glenmore Elementary School. One day my teacher brought in a couple of ice cream buckets full of quarters, dimes, nickels and pennies. She wanted to teach us about money that day. Our assignment was to match up the coins with coins that were marked out on paper with the amounts.

It was during this assignment that I figured that the teacher wouldn't notice if I put a few quarters in my pocket, so that's what I did. No one noticed my crime so I added a few more coins to my pockets. Soon both of my pockets were bulging and they jingled when I walked. I imagined all the candy I could buy with my new found fortune.

Needless to say my teacher took notice as it was obvious that I had coins in my pockets. I got into a little bit of trouble that day. My career as a thief didn't start out very well and much to my embarrassment I had to give the money back. The whole class was aware of what I did. My grandparents were notified after school and I ended up getting the belt on the bum that evening. It was too early in life to seek out my fortune I suppose. I was far from becoming a master thief because my strategy was flawed.

Somehow I needed to get my hands on some money. About a week after my attempted classroom caper I came up with another bright idea. After lunch instead of going to class I began to walk home. I was playing hooky and I had dollar signs in my eyes.

It took me about 45 minutes to walk home. Being aware of my grandpa's hidden key I located it and entered the house. I began to make a pitcher of

**Eric Badke**

Hawaiian Punch. My next task was to bring a small table and chair down to the end of the driveway, where I got myself set up. In an attempt to become wealthy, I was going to sell juice.

So I set up a table, a chair, and a pitcher of juice, some glasses, and a sign that was taped to the table. I sat there for about an hour and only one car had driven by. It wasn't a busy street by any means. I was beginning to feel hot and discouraged.

Finally another car approached and I began to anticipate a sale. It was my uncle Bill, my dad's older brother. To make a long story short he shut me down, much to my dismay. He came between me and my dreams to make some pocket money.

My short career of becoming a juice vendor was the topic of discussion at dinner that evening. My grandpa was chuckling about it but he began to roar with laughter after my uncle brought him the sign I had attached to my juice table earlier. It read: "Juice $1.99 a glass"

One evening after dinner, Shawn, Troy, Roland, and I were on the mountain just above the house. We were overturning rocks that were piled up. Much to our surprise a large snake quickly slithered out and coiled itself up on the path! Shawn and Troy's dad was nearby so we called him over to have a look. When he got there the snake began to hiss at us. He decided that the snake was dangerous so he killed it by hitting it on the head with a piece of steel rebar.

**Into The Dawn**

I found this snake to be fascinating. Even though they all urged me to leave it I picked it up and brought it home to show my grandma. She was busy in the kitchen doing the dishes. When I brought it in she screamed and told me to get it out of the house. She wasn't amused but I was.

I brought it to the garage and put it into a cardboard box. I was thinking that I should take the snake to school the next day for show-and-tell so that is what I did.

I was quite popular at school the next morning because everyone wanted to see the snake! A lot of kids were fascinated by its size. I kept it under my desk in the box during class and at lunch time I brought it out again.

This time though I dangled it around my neck and walked outside. Little girls were screaming as I walked by them so I proceeded to chase them around. They would scream and run away. It was fun as this snake was making me very popular that day especially with the girls.

At the end of the day after the school bus had dropped us off near our house I noticed that the snake was beginning to stink so I got rid of it by throwing it into a ditch. I was satisfied and had a great day with the snake. I would never forget it!

One sunny day, at school during the lunch hour, all the kids were outside playing around having fun on the playground. An adult supervisor came over to me and asked how I was doing.

**Eric Badke**

I ignored her question and countered, "You know what? I live in a cave up in that mountain!"

I pointed up at the mountain.

She reacted, "Really? What about your mom and dad?"

I told her that my dad lived in Vancouver and my mom lived in Penticton.

"Are you serious?" she asked concerned.

The next day while I was at school my dad, who was back visiting from university in Vancouver, received a knock at the door. Because of what I had told the supervisor the school had called social services. They came to inquire about my welfare. My dad was puzzled by this to say the least!

When I got home my dad asked me with wonder in his voice,

"Did you tell someone at your school that you live in a cave?" I had quite the imagination when I was young. I really wanted to live in a cave.

**Into The Dawn**

## Chapter 3

When I was eight years old, and my brother was seven, my dad received his teaching certificate from university and got a job as a primary school teacher in the mid-north sector of BC. Roland and I were excited that we were going to be back in our dad's life and we were moving to an Indian town.

We packed up our stuff and drove the seventeen hour trip from Kelowna north to our new home in Kitwanga. Kitwanga is a small lumber-milling town sixty miles between the larger towns of Smithers and Terrace. Kitwanga is separated by two sections: the village and the valley. The village was the reservation where all the natives lived and the valley was mainly white people. Both sections had a large lumber mill.

One amazing thing about the village was a row of totem poles that were hundreds of years old that were arrayed and faced away from the Skeena River that flowed past the village. Each pole had a story to tell.

Kitwangcool was another native community about ten miles east of Kitwanga. There is one interesting totem pole there. Near the base of the pole it has carved out of it a large oval shaped hole and fishermen with spears facing the hole carved around it. It told a hundred year old story about how the community had an especially cold winter one year. That year the hunting and fishing season didn't yield enough food to last the village during the long winter months. Towards the end of winter they were starving because they ran out of food. They were trying to cut a hole into the river ice to get at the fish but the ice was too thick much to their dismay. Without warning an angel appeared on the ice. Flames came from his hands and melted a hole in the ice so the people could get at the fish. The village was saved because of this event and they made a pole to commemorate it.

The valley, where we were going to live, had a mill, a mill pond, a store, a gas station, a small bank, a small medical clinic, a food take-out that had an arcade and pool table, and a large school where my dad was going to work. The school was large because the kids and teenagers that attended it came from the valley, the village, and Kitwangcool the neighboring reserve about ten miles away.

When we arrived in Kitwanga, Roland and I were excited to make new friends and explore the area. We moved into a three-bedroom trailer. Our dad took the room at the end and Roland and I had a bunk bed set up in the room next to our dad's. I took the top bunk and Roland took the bottom. As soon as we settled in our dad told us that he wanted to check out the national historic site called Battle Hill. The following description of this man-made 18th century earthward fortress is taken from Wikipedia.org.

*"Battle Hill, located in Kitwanga, was a fortress that utilized a strategic location, with a number of different defensive fortifications: things such as rocks and huge logs covered with spikes would roll down the sides of the slopes that surrounded the fortress during raids. [This fortress was defended by a legendary chief*

named Nekt. He was a warrior that wore a grizzly bear hide for protection which could not be penetrated by any weapons used by the enemy nations attacking. He used a number of weapons most notably a weapon called The One Strike Club to kill his enemy.] The Gitwangak people would drop back to this location during raids on the village in the lower part of the Gitwangak territory. This location was never lost during battle. The legends of the battles are recorded and passed on through oral history and passed on by the Gitwangak people.

The Gitxsan tribe has lived in this area for centuries. In the late 1700's, the Gitwangak warrior chief named Nekt decided that Battle Hill would make the perfect site for a fortified village. The steep sides would allow the homes on top to be easily protected. Nekt built his clan home here, along with that of two other clans.

Nekt was an aggressive warrior and led many successful raids against neighboring tribes to capture slaves, food stores, or ritual regalia. In retaliation, those tribes got together and attacked Battle Hill twice but were unsuccessful.

Nekt was eventually killed during one of his raids. He is remembered and celebrated by the Gitxsan people as a powerful and great leader"

After our dad told us about the hill we were excited to see it. We hopped into the car and made the five minute journey. It was a large hill and I was impressed that it was man made. I entered my imagination and visualized the battles that took place there almost 200

**Eric Badke**

years ago. I was fascinated that I was standing on a hill that held such historic significance. A large creek full of trout ran past and we were surrounded by snow-capped mountains. As we climbed down the hill I could imagine how numerous native warriors would attempt to climb up the hill to try and conquer the fort only to be met by a volley of arrows and rolling spiked logs. It was astonishing to think about.

Before we went home we stopped at the takeout and had burgers and fries. Our dad gave us a few quarters so we could play arcade games. This is where Roland and I met two kids that were our age named Shawn and Raymond. Their mom owned the takeout.

Shawn and Raymond would become our good friends and playmates. We would play ball tag and ride our bikes together. One day we constructed a large ramp out of wood. We would fly down a hill on our bikes, hit the ramp, and launch into the air, and hopefully, make a safe landing. It was quite the rush flying through the air like that and marking our landing distance. We would compete to see who could jump the farthest and risk scraping ourselves up if we didn't make a safe landing.

The morning after our first day in Kitwanga my dad told me that I was sleep walking again during the night. He told me that I opened the door to his bedroom and yelled,

"Daddy where's the money?"

**Into The Dawn**

I then closed the door and went back to bed. About fifteen minutes later I got out of bed again and opened my dad's door and told him,

"They are coming to take you away!"

He asked, "Who?"

I answered him,

"I am!"

I then closed the door and went back to bed again.

The three of us were quite amused when we talked about it over breakfast the next morning. That wouldn't be the last time I would sleep walk in that trailer. I also had numerous night terrors of which I wrote about earlier.

One day I was down at the mill pond skipping rocks into the water. A kid my age showed up and introduced himself as Ian. He was carrying a pump action BB gun rifle. If you pumped it up ten times or more it was a powerful gun. He pointed to a canoe that was overturned on the shore and asked if I wanted to go out in it with him. I asked him if it was okay to do that and he told me that all the kids go out in it.

So we got into the canoe and launched out towards the center of the pond. Ian began to pump up his BB gun and dipped the tip of the barrel into the water. He told me not to worry because it wasn't loaded. He pointed the air rifle at me and shot water into my face. I thought it was the coolest thing ever and I wanted to do the same to him! Amusing ourselves we did this to each other about five times.

Suddenly a flock of birds landed in a tree near the shore. As quick as he could Ian loaded his rifle with a BB projectile and gave it ten quick pumps. He then fired at the birds missing his mark.

"Your turn," he told me.

I loaded the gun and gave it ten quick pumps, took aim and fired. We took turns firing off pot shots at the birds missing them every time.

Out of nowhere a kid riding a motorbike showed up and was riding along the shore. We watched him for a bit, distracted, and then we returned to what we were doing. Ian now had the rifle. He pumped it up ten times, dipped it into the water, pointed it at me and shot me in the head with a BB! We'd both forgotten that I had loaded it.

When he shot me it felt like I was hit in the head with a log. All I could hear was a high pitched sound and as I hung my head over, I was dripping drops of blood profusely from my head wound into the water! We both panicked. I took off my shirt and held it to my head to soak up the blood.

To add to our distress Ian couldn't paddle the canoe to shore because a strong contrary wind was blowing. We were both very frightened and didn't know how badly I was hurt. Finally, after much struggle we made it to the shore. Once we pulled the canoe onto the beach I told

Ian that I would tell my dad that I fell on a rock. If he knew the truth we would both be in big trouble.

We went our separate ways and I headed for home with my head throbbing. When I got home I told my dad that my head was bleeding and that I slipped and fell on a rock. Immediately my dad took me to the community clinic so the doctor could examine me.

The jig was up when the doctor looked at my injury. If I fell on a rock the wound would have been jagged but that wasn't the case with my injury. The doctor called my dad over so he could have a look. It was a perfectly round hole where the BB made impact. My dad made me come clean about what truly happened and I told him the whole story. I had no other choice.

As a punishment for lying I was grounded and Ian's parents were notified. It's a good thing that the BB just bounced off of my skull and didn't impact any further. I could have been killed!

**Eric Badke**

## Chapter 4

When school started I was in Grade three and Roland was in Grade two. It just so happened that my dad was teaching a Grade 2-3 split class so Roland and I had our dad as our teacher. He was a great teacher since he made learning very fun. The only problem was that he was more severe with Roland and me than anyone else in the class. When we misbehaved in class (which was quite often because we were kids), when we got home he would discipline us by sending us to our rooms until dinner.

While at school I made a new friend. His name was John. We both liked the same type of rock music so after school he invited me over to his house so we could record radio music onto a cassette tape. While we were in the living room I told him that I was going to the bathroom. We were the only ones there at the time. On the way to the bathroom I noticed that John's sister's bedroom door was open. I felt curious and sneaky so I entered her room. As I entered her room I felt a surge of adrenaline shoot right through me because I knew I was doing something wrong. I was taking a monumental risk at getting caught!

I went over to her nightstand and opened the drawer. There were rolls of quarters and dimes in there. I decided that perhaps John's sister wouldn't notice if I took a roll of dimes worth $5. I quickly slipped the dimes into my pocket and returned to the living room where John was.

It was quite the caper and I thought I had gotten away with it until I purchased candy and brought it home. My dad caught me before I could sneak my ill-gotten gains into my bedroom. He asked me where I got the money to pay for the candy. I told him that I found the money but he didn't buy the story.

I knew I was caught so I told him the truth about what I did. I received a spanking and John's parents were contacted. Why was I always getting into trouble? My dad was very disappointed with me. That wasn't the last time I would get caught stealing.

During Christmas and summer holiday's we would drive from Kitwanga to Kelowna to visit our grandparents. It was during our second Christmas holiday visit that our dad met a woman named Joan. After we left Kelowna that Christmas our dad kept in contact with her. It wasn't until we returned to Kelowna the following summer that they decided to get married. Joan had two daughters named Kimberly and Christina. At the time of the marriage I was nine, Roland was eight, Kim was eight, and Christina was five. Since our family increased from three to six it was quite an adjustment to make.

**Eric Badke**

So we packed up their stuff into a large moving van and moved them up to Kitwanga. We moved into a town house for the first year of their marriage and then we all moved into a large house. I always hated moving because it seemingly took forever as there were so many boxes. In April 1983, two years after my parents got married; they had a baby boy and named him Matthew. He was a new addition to the family and he was adorable!

When I was ten and in Grade five, I became interested in a girl in my class. Her name was Bonnie and I found her to be quite cute with her long brown curly hair. It was during one of the school's lunch hour dances that I noticed I was attracted to her. The following week I saw her at a flea market. I wanted to buy her a gift so I bought her a small vile of perfume and nervously gave it to her. If I had it my way I would have showered her with many gifts. I had a schoolboy crush on her and couldn't get her out of my mind. A couple of days later I wrote her a note. In it I asked her if she liked me and to check one of two boxes: yes or no. She returned the note to me and she checked, yes. My heart skipped a beat and I was exhilarated at her answer. I wanted her to be my girlfriend so I wrote her another note asking her if she wanted to be my date at the next Friday night school dance. She replied yes.

I asked my dad for some money so I could take Bonnie to the dance. He thought about it for a moment and then he told me that if I picked him some Shaggy Mane wild mushrooms he would give me ten cents for each mushroom I picked. I then proceeded outside to get busy picking. About an hour later I had enough to pay for the dance.

The big night came and I met Bonnie at the dance. We had a great time and it was an honor to be her date. I loved dancing with her, especially to the slow songs. She became my first girlfriend and we soon fell into puppy love and continued to write notes to each other.

Unfortunately, our relationship fizzled out the next summer when I left with my family on our holidays, but I will never forget our time as boyfriend-girlfriend. We were too young and innocent to be kissing but we would walk around school holding hands, she loved me, and I would never forget it.

**Eric Badke**

# Chapter 5

The memories that I am going to write about next are tough for me. It says in the Bible to honor your mother and father, but I think it is important to write about this because it is a point of reference as to why my life became so difficult in my teens, and well into my 20s. These days I harbor no negative feelings towards my parents. I love them both very much and wish the best for both of them. There are reasons why these circumstances took place, even though at the time I couldn't understand why. I chalk it up mostly to the fact that it was a time of confusion for both me and my parents, who were in their early 30s. We were all still learning and growing.

Life began to decline for Roland and me two years after the marriage, but mostly for me. The first time my dad hit me was when I was eleven. My new step-sister Christina was being a pest so I pushed her away from me. My dad saw what I did and rushed me. He pummeled me with his fists in the face and head.

Awhile later he told me that he had every right to hit me and I believed him. Not knowing that it was against the law for parents to punch their kids, I had no reason not to believe him. Over time, the periods between beatings began to diminish as it became a regular ordeal.

The next event took place just after I turned thirteen. One evening after dinner my stepmom, who I will call mom from this point on, offered me a job as the dishwasher for the family. She would pay me one dollar every time I would perform this task. I agreed to do it. After about a week I noticed that this job was quite difficult for me for various reasons. When my mom cooked dinner she managed to use almost every dish in the house and it would take me almost an hour-and-a-half to wash, dry, and put them away. I also noticed that after dinner the rest of the family would enjoy a time of leisure, either watching a fun program on TV or outside on the lawn playing badminton. I was stuck in the kitchen doing a mountain of dishes while everyone else was having fun and I didn't think it was fair.

One evening I had enough of it. Halfway into doing the dishes I decided to quit, so I left my duty as the dishwasher and I joined my family who were watching TV in the living room. My mom asked me what I was doing so I told her that I was quitting my job as dishwasher.

"Oh no, you're not!" she said.

I replied that it wasn't fair and it wasn't worth the dollar a day she was paying me. She got up and walked over to me, grabbed me by my hair and dragged me to my feet. It hurt very much. Now that I was on my feet she began to push me toward the kitchen. I told her to leave me alone and then she took a swing at me and hit me in the jaw!

"Leave me alone!" I exclaimed.

She continued to come at me and now we were in the kitchen. A commercial came on the TV so my dad got up from the couch to come and break up what was happening. When my mom saw that my dad was

**Eric Badke**

coming, she flung herself to the floor as if I hit her! I couldn't believe it! My dad took the bait believing that I had apparently hit her and he charged at me and began to punch me with his fists. I could see stars as he hit me and I fell to the floor. He continued to batter me until he was satisfied. After he finished he told me to go to my room. As I was walking to my room I noticed that there were bruises forming and also several small pieces from a newly-chipped tooth in my mouth.

So there I was in my room sitting on my bed feeling very unfortunate to say the least. My circumstances were bleak and seemingly unrelenting. I was angry and I wanted revenge in the worst way. How was I going to get back at my parents for how they were treating me?

I sat there and contemplated this for about twenty minutes until it came to me. My mom and dad had high hopes that I would one day become a model citizen in the community. I decided that I would shatter those high hopes that my parents had for me. I would become a burglar.

# Chapter 6

I want you to know that at this point in my life I didn't care about any consequences that would result from any of my actions. My life was cheap to me I didn't even want to be alive because of what was happening. I decided that the next evening I would begin my stint as a night burglar so I mentally prepared myself all the next day for what I was about to do.

At that time of year it got dark at around 5 p.m. so that was an advantage for me. If a house had the lights off that would indicate to me that nobody would be home at that particular dwelling. After dinner I went to my room and took stock of what I would need. I concluded that all I would need was three items: a pack sack, a flashlight, and some gloves. I would also need a lot of courage because what I was about to do was crazy. I figured why not just go out and survey the scene? If it didn't look good I would abort the mission and come back home, simple as that.

So I grabbed what I needed and went out into the cold winter night. I would begin with my neighborhood so at the end of my driveway I took a right. I remember the crunch of my winter boots on the snow as I continued down the road towards my new destiny as a night thief.

The first house I came upon had lights on and so did the second so I bypassed those and continued on. The third house I saw looked vacant as there were no lights on. I felt a surge of adrenalin flow through me as I continued my stride up the driveway towards the house. This was crazy! I looked all around and down the main road making sure there was no one around or cars coming to notice me.

I figured that I would ring the doorbell first and if someone answered I would tell them I was looking for my lost dog, then ask them if they had seen him or not. I figured the plan was sound.

So I went to the door and rang the bell to see if anyone was home. Nobody came to the door so I rang the bell a couple more times. Satisfied that there was nobody home I tried the doorknob. It wasn't locked! I was now at a crossroad and I had a decision to make as to whether I would go in or not. If I got caught I would be in big trouble. If I went in I would be taking a big chance as the owner of the house could come home at any moment! I decided to take a chance. In reality I didn't care if I got caught so I had nothing to lose. I went in.

As I entered the house my heart was beating rapidly in my chest and my breathing was shallow and heavy. I turned on my mini flashlight and bypassed the kitchen and swiftly went for the bedroom. I decided that I would just have a look and I didn't want to take anything that would make it obvious to the owner that there was a break-in.

I entered the bedroom and had a look in the nightstand drawers. There was nothing of value in them so I went to the closet and opened the bi-fold doors. Bingo! On the floor of the closet was a large wide-mouthed wine jug full of change, mostly quarters! There must have been $50 worth of quarters in there!

**Into The Dawn**

I wanted to stick to my guns though about not creating suspicion, so I only took about $10 worth and left the rest. I stood up and peered down at the wine jug. Satisfied that the owner wouldn't notice that he had been robbed I headed towards the front door so I could make my exit.

Once outside I nervously made my way down the driveway towards the main road. Once on the road I knew I was in the clear. I didn't get caught! The rush that I felt from having my first successful mission was unexplainable. I felt on top of the world! I now had money to play arcade games and buy snacks at the take-out.

Now that I had accomplished my first mission as a night burglar I was hooked. I had a new addiction to the adrenaline that I experienced performing the act; the reward of the booty I received, and the rush from getting away with the crime.

Within the next week I broke into two more houses and took nothing that would cause suspicion. I was only able to acquire some loose change.

The fourth house that I broke into was a monumental risk. I must have been out of my mind to go in there as I knew that it was a biker's house. No one appeared to be home so I went in. Immediately I noticed that there was a variety of mini bottles of liquor on top of the TV about twenty in all. Figuring that they wouldn't notice if I took four of them, I put them in my bag, and continued into the bedroom.

**Eric Badke**

I had a look in the closet and found a fancy-looking case. When I opened it I was in shock! The case contained a genuine 44 mag Desert Eagle pistol! It was large and menacing. I studied that hand cannon and it intimidated me to say the least. What was I doing in this house? I definitely wasn't going to take that gun, so I closed the case, put it back where it was, and left the house in a hurry.

That Friday night I was hanging with my friends at the take-out. There were girls there that I wanted to impress so I took out the mini liquor bottles and showed it to the group. They asked me where I got the booze and I told them it was a secret. Wanting to be the life of the party I told them I could get more; enough to get the whole group of us drunk. They told me to go for it. For courage I drank two mini bottles and left the other two with my buddies.

Now that I had a buzz going, I made my way back to the biker's house. All the lights were off. I knocked on the door and there was no answer. I tried the door and it wasn't locked so I went in, adrenaline surging!

What I was about to do was insane but I desperately wanted to impress my friends. I went to the TV and grabbed all the mini bottles of liquor and then made a quick exit. I knew that I had now crossed a threshold and the owner of the house would know for sure that he had been burglarized.

Twenty minutes later I was back amongst my friends and I started passing out bottles. I now had a new level of respect from them which made it a mission accomplished as far as I was concerned.

We all lived in a small town so it wasn't surprising that word got out from the owners of the house that they were burglarized. The police were brought in and they began an investigation. All they had to go on was the tread design from my shoes that I left behind on their floor.

Since the wife of the biker worked the till at the General Store whenever a teen would come in she would ask to check the bottom of their shoes. I was getting very edgy as things were beginning to close in on me. I was not in a very good position to say the least!

About a week later the police showed up at my house. Word had got out that I had stolen those mini-booze bottles and I was caught. Busted!

The police told my parents that the biker wouldn't press charges if he was repaid for what was stolen. They also wanted me to go over to their house and apologize.

The next day, after school, my parents and I drove to the biker's house and once we arrived we were invited in. I couldn't believe this was happening. It was a scary situation, I felt awkward, and embarrassed. Regardless of my apology the biker said that if he had his way he would take me outside and tan my hide. His wife was against that, much to my relief.

So now that it was known in the community about what I did, my parents decided it would be best if I left town

**Eric Badke**

for a while. They would send me to Kelowna to live with my grandparents and attend high school there.

So I packed up my stuff, and my dad with mom in the passenger seat, drove me to the highway gas station where the Greyhound bus picks up passengers. I was both anxious and excited at the idea of beginning a new life in Kelowna and attending a new high school. Once I boarded I was deep in thought as the bus travelled down the highway towards my new destiny.

About 150 kilometers into my trip the bus stopped at a small town and took on a new passenger. He took the seat next to mine at the back of the bus. He was in his mid-fifties. He introduced himself to me and pulled out a twenty-six ounce bottle of Southern Comfort from his pack sack. He twisted the lid off, took a swig and passed it to me. Reluctantly, I accepted the bottle, put it to my lips, and took a swig.

It burned my throat as the liquid went down and provided me with a warm feeling in my chest. It felt and tasted very good. We passed the bottle back and forth and it didn't take long before I was fully intoxicated. I was having a pleasurable time and I felt like an adult. This was the first time I had ever drank this much alcohol and been this drunk before!

The man began to pass the bottle around to the other passengers who were in the back of the bus and before long it became a party. Eventually the bus driver pulled in and made a stop at a gas station that had all the lights off indicating that it was closed. He put the bus in park and made his way towards us at the back of the bus. He came to the man that was sitting with me and told him firmly to get off the bus. The man began to protest and ask why. The bus driver replied,

"You know why!"

The bus driver grabbed the man, pulled him to his feet, and began shoving him down towards the front of the bus. By this time my head was swimming with inebriation. I yelled out,

"Let him stay!"

All the other passengers as well as the bus driver took notice at my drunken outburst, turned around, and looked at me.

Eventually the man was ejected from the bus into the cold winter night, stranded. It was a good thing I looked my age of thirteen or else I probably would have been kicked off as well. I think it was the grace of God that kept me on that bus that evening.

Finally the bus arrived in Prince George and we had a two hour layover. As I was sitting in the terminal I began to feel queasy and everything was spinning. I hardly made it to the bathroom before I proceeded to vomit into a toilet. Full of regret at drinking that alcohol I made my way back to the waiting room and took my seat.

After it was announced over the loud speaker that my bus was now boarding, I got onto the bus and continued on with the journey. I fell asleep and when I woke up in the morning we had arrived in Kelowna. I

**Eric Badke**

was in rough shape as I was now experiencing my first hangover.

**Into The Dawn**

## Chapter 7

My grandpa was waiting for me at the Kelowna terminal and I was happy to see him.

I don't have a large amount of interesting stories about my six month stay in Kelowna. I will just say that the school I attended, Kelowna Secondary School (KSS), was very big and interesting. There were predominantly two groups of teenagers that attended that school: the thrashers and the preps.

These two groups were always at odds with each other and rumbles would ensue from time to time. You could always tell who was from what group by the way they dressed. The thrashers would have long hair along with studded bracelets and jackets. The preps would dress moderately. Not long after I began attending KSS I identified myself with the thrashers. I started listening to heavy metal music and quite frequently a group of us would cut school to go shoplifting at the Woolworths department store.

We would go to the music department and when the clerk wasn't looking we would grab and conceal cassette tapes in our jackets. We would then sell the tapes for $5 to other students at the school. Shoplifting would make me feel rebellious and I prided myself at never getting caught.

I lived a privileged lifestyle while living with my grandparents. My grandma was a very good cook. If I needed money and a ride to go to the arcade they would sometimes provide it. The only thing that we were at odds about was that I enjoyed going out for walks at night but my grandma wouldn't let me.

"There are evil things in the night!" she told me.

Whenever I wanted to go out at night grandma would stand between me and the door blocking my way. I would have to physically remove her so I could make a swift exit into the night. I was very disrespectful in my youth from time to time and there is no excuse for treating my grandma in this way.

One evening I was going stir crazy and had a strong desire to go out. There was a sliding door that led to the TV room and because I knew my grandma would strongly protest my going out, I ended up locking her in. I then went out. My grandpa wasn't home at the time. I walked to the main road and began hitch-hiking into town.

A couple of friends of mine from school, who were getting a ride into town from their mom, stopped to pick me up. We got dropped off at the park and once we arrived at a table they produced a mickey of whiskey. We passed the bottle around until it was depleted then we sat around smoking cigarettes and socializing. I felt in my element behaving in this way. I felt like an adult drinking alcohol and smoking cigarettes with my friends but I had crossed the line with my grandparents. Eventually I would have to go home and face the music.

After I hitch-hiked home my grandparents were waiting for me and were very upset. They told me that they had called my parents and that they were sending me back home. I then felt very remorseful for what I had done. I didn't want to go back to Kitwanga but I didn't have a choice in the matter.

They then put me on a bus and I reluctantly travelled the seventeen-hour trip north to Kitwanga. I was almost home when I noticed that my ears were plugged. I closed my mouth, plugged my nose with my fingers, and then attempted to unplug my ears by blowing air through them. Something popped and all of a sudden one of my ears began to throb with pain. I had a terrible earache for the remainder of the trip.

**Eric Badke**

## Chapter 8

I didn't receive a warm reception from my parents when I arrived home. On the contrary, they were very upset with me for how I treated my grandmother. They searched my bags and found a Sony Walkman that I had shoplifted and a lock-blade knife that I purchased on the black market. I couldn't give an account for where I had acquired these items so I told them the truth.

My dad yelled at me and told me I was grounded. I was in their bedroom when this went down.

"Get out of here!" my dad yelled.

As he pushed me towards the door he shoved me off my feet and I fell, hitting my head on the corner of a travel trunk that was on the floor. The impact caused a gash on my scalp that began to soak my hair with blood. I curled up into a ball and cupped my throbbing wound with my hand. Unaware of what he did to me my dad began to kick me, telling me to get out of his room.

I got up and blood dripped from the laceration on my scalp to the floor. My eyes were also wet with tears from the pain I was experiencing. My mom grabbed a towel and I placed it on my injury to apply pressure and soak up the blood.

My parents then drove me to the hospital that was in Hazelton, thirty miles away. I needed to get stitches. Before the doctor could stitch me up he had to freeze the wound. When he inserted the needle into my scalp

I felt pain like I have never felt before. It made me cry out in agony!

When we got home I went to my bed. I now had a stitched-up wound and a terrible earache from the bus trip to contend with.

The next day I went to school, and when I got home my dad was installing a lock on the outside of my bedroom door. He told me that for the two weeks of grounding I would be locked in my room from the time I got home from school until it was time to go back to school in the morning. They would serve me supper and I would have to eat it in my room.

I felt that this punishment was very unconventional indeed. After a week of serving out my sentence, I decided to rebel. One day I didn't come home after school until it was dinner time. When I got home my dad told me that I had an extra two weeks added to my sentence for not coming home from school. Before he locked me in my room he punched me in the face to reinforce what he was telling me.

I had had enough of the abuse I was receiving from my dad. I decided while I was in metal work class at school I would make a knife. I vowed to myself that if my dad hit me one more time I would stab him.

After school I went home and I had my knife with me. My dad locked me in my room again and I stashed my weapon under some clothing that I had on the floor.

About a half an hour later I needed to go to the bathroom so I proceeded to knock on the door hoping my dad would let me out. I kept knocking but my dad didn't come to unlock me. I then became angry and began to pound on the door. I must have annoyed my dad because all of a sudden the door opened and I received a punch in the face!

An instant after he hit me I lunged towards where I had my knife stashed and I attempted to grab it. My dad must have known something was up because he charged and pounced on me before I could get the knife in hand. He then restrained me and searched around under my clothes and found the knife. He dragged me to the middle of the bedroom, rolled me over on my back, and sat on top of my chest to hold me down. He then told my brother to call the police.

I begged my dad to get off of me because the weight of him on my chest was restricting my breathing. I was panicking because I was suffocating and my dad wouldn't get off me no matter how much I pleaded with him!

My brother came back very scared and told my dad he couldn't get a hold of the police. My dad told him to call a couple of teachers that he worked with at the school. About fifteen minutes later a couple of teachers showed up to witness this ominous scene. They were wide-eyed and didn't really know why they were there. I could tell that they were confused and didn't want to get involved.

It wasn't long afterwards when the scene became defused and my dad finally got off me, he left the room and locked the door behind him. I was in the depths of despair. I needed out.

The next day after school I didn't come home until bedtime. When I got home my dad had the front door locked and no matter how much I knocked he wouldn't let me in. It was towards the end of winter and it was freezing outside. I was desperately cold and scared. I had no other choice than to sleep in the family van.

I attempted to sleep but my shivering was out of control. I couldn't handle it so I left the van and decided to walk to my friend's house. He let me in and I was able to stay the night on the floor of his bedroom. He and his mom became aware of what was going on in my household because I had confided with them about it once I arrived.

**Eric Badke**

# Chapter 9

The next day during school I was called to the office by the secretary. The principal and the vice-principal wanted to talk to me. It turns out that they knew of what was going on at our family home. They informed me that I was going to be placed in a group home in Prince Rupert. They also told me that my new social worker was at my home picking up my belongings from the house to bring to my new home.

I was relieved that I wouldn't have to go back to live with my parents anymore. I wasn't the perfect son by any means but I felt that I never did anything that justified what they did to me.

So my new social worker drove me the two-and-a-half-hour trip to Prince Rupert.

*Prince Rupert is a port city in the province of British Columbia, Canada. Located on Kaien Island, Prince Rupert is the land, air, and water transportation hub of British Columbia's North Coast, and has a population of 12,508 people (Wikipedia)*

When I arrived at the group home in Prince Rupert I got settled in. I met a youth my age who was also a resident at the group home and his name was Brad. He would be my roommate.

The facilitator of the home gave me $10 for my allowance, so after dinner Brad brought me downtown to go to the Hot Spot arcade. He told me that I should use half of the $10 to purchase a marijuana joint from one of the dealers at the arcade. I agreed and gave him the money so he could go score. I had never been high before so this was going to be a new experience for me.

After Brad scored I followed him out into the back alley and he lit it up. He took a toke and passed to me. He told me to inhale the smoke and hold it in.

After one puff I began to feel the effects of the drug. This was new territory for me and it felt like I entered a different realm. I didn't know what to expect. My reality definitely became altered and it kind of startled me. I didn't know it would be like that. After one more toke I had had enough and told Brad he could finish it.

I was stoned for the first time and I was ambivalent as to whether I was enjoying myself or not.

"Are you high man?" he said.

"Oh yeah," I replied.

"Let's go play some video games!" he said with a grin on his lit-up face.

Living at the group home was definitely an improvement from living with my parents in Kitwanga. I was free to be who I wanted to be and I was no longer living under tyranny.

I was enrolled in the high school and I began attending classes regularly, although I did continue my habit of skipping classes and going downtown to shoplift from time to time.

**Eric Badke**

The following Friday after I moved in I received another $10 for my allowance. Brad came to me with an idea. He told me that he could get some acid. I asked him what that was. He told me that it was a blotter of acid on a small square piece of paper that would cause us to hallucinate and laugh. He told me it would cost $10 for a hit.

I decided that I would give it a try so we walked to a house and I gave him my money. He went into the house with my money and his. About five minutes later he came out and produced a couple of small square pieces of thick paper wrapped in tin foil. We both unwrapped the tin; we popped the square piece of paper into our mouths, and swallowed it down. I could taste the acid in my mouth. He told me it would be about an hour before the drug would take effect.

"Let's go to the Hot Spot!" he exclaimed.

"Let's go!" I agreed.

I couldn't think of a better place to be when I achieved the high.

So we arrived at the Hot Spot and about fifteen minutes later Brad told me that he had to go meet a girl and that he would see me at home. He bid me farewell and told me to have fun. I couldn't believe he was leaving me. I didn't have any money left so I just watched other people play video games waiting for the acid to kick in.

After about an hour into my anticipation I still didn't feel the effects of the drug. I surrendered to the fact that perhaps what I took was bunk and it wasn't going to work.

About ten minutes later though in one fell swoop it hit me!

The music on the juke box seemingly began to slow down and it felt like I was slowly falling to the floor but I wasn't. I turned around from watching people play video games and I looked at a couple of men playing pool. Their heads were indented and enlarged to epic proportions! The top of their heads were three times larger than normal and their noses were sucked in deforming their appearance even more.

I began to walk across the room and I looked down. The carpet design at the arcade was in motion and appeared to be transformed into slithering snakes!

"I have to get out of here!" I told myself.

I felt deranged and giddy. I exited the arcade and entered into the dark nightlife of the city. Sounds were amplified and altered. Everyone I looked at had deformed enlarged heads with indented noses.

I saw a police cruiser drive by and I instantly wondered if they knew I was high.

My mind would begin to wander and then I would come to my senses; my mind would wander yet again and then I would come to my senses yet again. This was outlandish! My reality was once again altered messing with my sanity. Somehow though, it was an amazing experience and I was having a good time.

**Eric Badke**

I came to a long bridge and began to walk across it. I walked and I walked and I walked some more. It seemed like the bridge was never ending! I looked ahead of me and I looked behind me and it was the same distance. I kept walking and walking, tripping out that I wasn't gaining any ground on this never-ending bridge! Finally, much to my relief, I came to the end of the bridge.

I was keeping my composure and going out of my mind at the same time.

After my epic journey on the road I made it home. I went in and Brad was sitting on the couch watching TV. As soon as he saw me a smirk came across his face. He grabbed his cigarettes and we headed outside. As soon as we closed the front door behind us we both burst into an uncontrollable fit of laughter! His hilarity was making me laugh and my hilarity was making him laugh. I was laughing so hard that my sides began to hurt!

Soon we calmed down and I asked him,

"How long is this going to last?"

He told me ten hours. Ten hours? We were going to be up all night!

Because we didn't want our facilitators to suspect anything, we went to the room that we shared and closed the door. He put some Pink Floyd on the stereo and we laid back and tripped out on the tunes.

**Into The Dawn**

This was quite the occurrence as we were thoroughly enjoying ourselves. I surmised that it was well worth the $10 we spent on it.

**Eric Badke**

# Chapter 10

About two months later, the year 1986, after my fourteenth birthday, my social worker visited me in Prince Rupert. He came to me with an offer. He presented me with an opportunity to enter into a coed program for youths who were on the verge of getting into trouble. He told me it was a six-month program where I could gain some life skills and receive counseling.

I figured, why not? I had no reason to doubt that it would be a good experience for me.

This program, called Keweetin, was located in the isolated woods outside of the northern BC town of Fort St John. It was on an old ranch that was renovated to suit the needs of the clients that stayed there.

So I packed up my stuff and my social worker drove me from Prince Rupert to Hazelton. There was a staff member from Keweetin who lived in Hazelton. He would drive me up to Fort St John where I would be enrolled into the program.

Once we arrived at Keweetin it looked a lot different than how I envisioned it. It had four main buildings: a bunk building, a dining building, a small school, and a recreation building. It also had an outhouse and a sauna.

I don't really have much to write about my time at Keweetin other than that it was beneficial. At any given time there would be eight teenage boys and eight teenage girls of varying ages attending the program.

We really cared for one another as we could relate and empathize with each other. We would hug each other a lot.

That winter we had an opportunity to go on a road trip to Jasper to go cross-country skiing at Angel Glacier. It was amazing. We got to experience the beauty of God's creation while trekking on our skis within the valleys of the Rocky Mountains. I will never forget it.

There is another occurrence that happened to me after we got back from our trip that I will never forget.

At 7:30 every morning, before breakfast, it was mandatory for us to jog (or walk) two miles in order to get some exercise. We would go out into the dark of the morning one mile down the road to the marker and then turn around and come back. All we had were the stars and the moon to light our way. Because of my asthma I would usually walk the two miles.

One morning I was walking in the dark on my way back to the homestead. I saw a light and I thought a car was coming around the corner. All of a sudden night became brighter than day as all my surroundings were lit up! This light that was coming from above me made me flinch. The road was lit up and so was the ditch!

I looked up and saw a spotlight that was coming from the clouds, alighting on me and me only! The clouds were also rippling with beautiful colors that bedazzled me. What was going on? This light eventually began to move behind the mountain and the rippling colors on the clouds moved with it, then it disappeared and it became dark again.

**Eric Badke**

What was that?

It couldn't have been a helicopter or else I would have heard it! Was it a UFO? I highly doubt it!

What I like to think as I look back on this memory was that it was a possibility that God shone a spotlight on me from the heavens to let me know that He considered me, that he loved me, that He had a genuine concern for me, as He does for all His children.

At the time of this event I walked away from it in confusion. What did this mean? I was so perplexed at what had happened to me that morning. It definitely wasn't a normal occasion. If it was God manifesting Himself to me from the clouds I do feel very fortunate indeed!

After my six-month stay at Keweetin I graduated from the program and it was time to leave. I was very sad to leave all my friends behind as I considered them to be family.

## Chapter 11

After Keweetin I was placed in a group home in Smithers B.C., sixty miles south of Kitwanga. As soon as I got there I was introduced to a gentleman named Steve. He was going to be my child-care worker. Steve was a carpenter and he began to take me to work with him.

I wasn't getting paid but I respected Steve. I was learning how to work, and was gaining experience.

He asked me if I wanted to spend the summer working with him at a wilderness fishing camp called the Silver Hilton, up the Babine River. I accepted the offer, and a couple of days later we drove to the river where we met the pilot who was going to launch the motor boat. The three of us loaded the boat with provisions then we set off. This was exciting because we were now going down the river at high speed.

The pilot of the boat knew the river and where to avoid the rocks. Steve and I relaxed as the boat sped through tree-lined canyons and beautiful mountains towering on both sides of the fast-flowing river. There were many places to stop and fish but we were on a mission to get to the lodge before dinner so we kept going.

After about three hours we arrived at the Silver Hilton and met up with the owner of the camp and his wife as we unloaded the boat of its supplies. The pilot of the speed boat happened to be their son.

This camp consisted of a large main lodge facing the river, four cabins that housed six beds each, a shed, an airstrip, and a sauna.

Avid sports fishermen would come up from the States and pay $1,500 a week to stay at the camp and fish the river for award-winning steel head salmon. At the end of the week they would have the option to river-raft the rapids eighty kilometers (fifty miles) down the river back to civilization and then catch a flight back home.

That evening I settled into the cabin I was sharing with Steve. While Steve read a book I spent about a half an hour killing mosquitoes before we turned off the light and went to sleep.

The next day after breakfast they put me to work. My task was to rake all the rocks off the airstrip so that planes could land safely with the clients. It was a monumental task that would take a few days.

About a couple hours into my labor a small, three-seat, bubble-style helicopter landed at the camp. I kept working until my new boss, the owner of the camp, called me over. He told me that we were going helicopter fishing which sounded very exciting indeed! I had never been up in a helicopter before!

So we loaded in the fishing rods and tackle, then the pilot, my boss, and I got into the helicopter and we took off!

It was sensational taking off and rising into the sky like that. It wasn't long before we were hundreds of feet in the air and the wilderness was far below us. The rotors were so loud that we had to communicate with each other through our headsets!

We coasted along for about ten minutes before we landed beside a lake on the top of a mountain.

After we got out of the helicopter, my boss gave me a crash course on fly-fishing and then we began to cast our lines where a stream was feeding into the lake. It took only a half a minute before I had a trout on the line. Within a half an hour we had about eight trout each. It was amazing fishing this untouched lake on the top of this mountain!

That night we had battered, pan-fried trout for dinner and it was delicious!

I spent about a month working at the Silver Hilton. I learned how to work hard and I gained a few skills.

It was a pleasure to have the opportunity to go fishing and river-rafting during our free time in the cool of the evening. When it was time to go home, I now had to travel up the river at high speed back to a different reality: my life back in the group home.

**Eric Badke**

# Chapter 12

The following April my social worker decided that it was time for me to go home and try living with my parents again. Another reason for me to move back home was that my family was getting set to move from Kitwanga south to the Fraser Valley. My dad got a job as a teacher at Seabird Island, which is a native reserve just outside of Agassiz.

The year was 1987 and I was fifteen when I moved back home. For the time being life wasn't too bad living with my parents.

After the school year ended we packed up all our stuff into a large moving van, said goodbye to Kitwanga, and drove to our new two story house in Agassiz.

As we moved into the new house my dad informed the family that this would be a new start for us and as a family we were encouraged at this thought.

**Into The Dawn**

After we moved into the house we all got into our van to travel west. We were beginning our summer holiday by attending a Baha'i summer camp at Shawinigan Lake on Vancouver Island.

Going across on the ferry from Vancouver to Victoria is always a good experience as the scenery and the fresh ocean air is very invigorating for the soul.

Once we arrived at Shawinigan Lake summer camp Roland and I made a few new friends. There was a beautiful, blond-haired girl named Ange who I became very interested in. One of the activities of the camp for young people included a ballroom dancing class. Ange was chosen to become my partner and we had fun together learning how to dance.

A week later, on the last evening of summer camp, a group of us teens were down by the lake socializing and listening to music on a portable stereo. Eventually my dad showed up on the hill that was above the beach area and yelled out, informing Roland and me that we were leaving. Everyone in the group knew that there was chemistry between Ange and me.

"We want to see you kiss her goodbye!" they cried.

I asked, "What does she want?"

All of a sudden I became bold. She was watching me as I walked towards her and I noticed that she had a sparkle in her eye. I bent down and gave her a long, soulful kiss. It lasted half a minute, and for those thirty seconds I was in heaven!

**Eric Badke**

She was very beautiful and out of my league, so I felt very fortunate in those precious moments!

After the kiss, my buddies were giving me high fives and fist bumps. We said our goodbyes and we left. I was sad with the thought that I would never see her again.

As it turned out, my dad informed us that after the camp ended we were going to the town of Courtney to stay with friends on their farm for about a week. Ange lived in Courtney!!

The night we arrived at our dad's friend's house I got Ange's phone number and called her to tell her I was in the area. She was as overjoyed as was I.

Ange and I spent a romantic week getting to know each other better and we created many good memories together. When it was time to go back to Agassiz with my family I was heartbroken. I made the mistake of falling in love with Ange and it took me a long time to get over her. But as the old saying goes: "It is better to have loved and lost than to not have loved at all."

# Chapter 13

When the new school year began in September I was placed in an alternate school because I had already failed Grade 8 twice. I enjoyed going to that school because we were allowed to drink coffee and listen to music while we did our school work.

One evening my mom and I were having a lengthy heart to heart conversation. Toward the end of the talk, she told me that if I was ever in a situation with my friends where there was drinking involved and I got drunk, she would understand and that it would be okay as long as I didn't come home that night.

We hugged it out, felt love towards each other, and that was the end of our discussion.

Lo and behold a circumstance did come up one weekend when I was with my friends and we were drinking. I remembered what my mom had said so I stayed the night at a friend's place, thinking that would be okay.

The next evening I decided to go home and when I got there the door was locked! I rang the doorbell but no one came. I went to the side of the house and looked in the window. I saw most of my family sitting in the rec room watching TV. I knew something was up. I also knew how to get into the house through the bathroom window. Once inside I went into the TV room.

My dad asked me, "What are you doing here?"

**Eric Badke**

"I live here," I answered.

"No you don't," he responded. "What makes you think you could stay out all night?"

I was shocked. "Mom told me that if I was ever in a situation that I was drinking, it would be okay, just not come home that night."

"I said no such thing!" my mom retorted. "You are a liar!"

I couldn't believe my ears! What betrayal! I was so angry!

That circumstance forced me to leave the family home. I went back into foster care. My new social worker placed me into a foster home in Yarrow, which is a small farming community about twenty-five kilometers (15 miles) from Chilliwack.

My foster parents' names were Terri and Don. They lived in a small house with one bedroom and a back room where there was a washer, dryer, and a bunk bed where I would be staying with my foster brother Jimmy. They had three show dogs and two cats.

When I moved in I didn't have my asthma inhaler, which made a bad situation even worse. After about an hour inside the house all the animal dander that was floating around triggered within me a full-on asthma attack! This wouldn't be the first time, as I grew up with asthma and had countless attacks previous to this, but this was bad!

**Into The Dawn**

*No one really knows what causes asthma. What we do know is that asthma is a chronic inflammatory disease of the airways. The causes of asthma symptoms can vary from person to person. Still, one thing is consistent with asthma: when airways come into contact with an asthma trigger, the airways become inflamed, narrow, and fill with mucus.*

*When you have an asthma attack, spasms of the muscles around the airways, inflammation and swelling of the mucosal membrane lining the airways, and excessive amounts of mucus contribute to airway narrowing. This makes airway resistance increase and the work of breathing more difficult, causing shortness of breath, cough, and wheezing. You may have coughing with asthma because of the irritation inside the airway and the body's attempt to clean out the accumulations of thick mucus. (Webmd.com)*

I was suffering intolerably because I was wheezing terribly and could barely catch a breath. It would take every muscle in my upper torso to get a breath in. My face was turning blue and I ended up on the floor as a frightened Terri called an ambulance.

When it arrived the paramedics put me on oxygen. Finally, after a few minutes I could breathe again, much to my relief. I was brought to the hospital and they kept me there for a couple of days. They issued me a new inhaler.

After the hospital I went back to Yarrow to live with Terri, Don and Jimmy. Jimmy was a good-looking teen about my age. He introduced me to a couple of his other friends named Wally and Chris.

As a group we would go out almost every day and break into people's homes. In total, we probably broke into about twenty houses. At the time it was exciting and whenever we scored money we would split it up and spend it at the arcade.

One time when Jimmy and I were out scamming, we came upon a Can-Am dirt bike that was in a garage. No one was home at the house so I decided to fire it up. Jimmy hopped on the back and we took off at high speed. This was a very powerful bike! We took it to the dike that aligned the river. We burned around on the bike at top speed up and down the road that was on top of the dike. Looking back on it now I realized how reckless we were. After we were finished our joy ride we ended up quietly pushing the bike back into the garage and then went home.

Another day Jimmy and I went out looking for a house to break into on the outskirts of Yarrow. We found a dwelling that appeared unoccupied. Jimmy went in through a window in the basement and came up to open the back door. He told me that maybe we shouldn't rob this house because it looked like whoever lived there were people we shouldn't mess around with.

Despite that, we went into the basement. Jimmy pointed to a bench press that had a lot of weight on it, at least two-hundred-and-fifty pounds. I knew right away what he meant when he told me that we shouldn't mess with these people, but I was stubborn so we continued up the stairs.

After going through the bedrooms we took some men's jewelry and about $30 in change. Later that day we bought some marijuana off of one of the dealers in town, paying for it with the change that we just scored.

The next night I came home at around ten. Terri and Don greeted me with serious expressions on their face. They told me that two truckloads of men came to the house earlier looking for me. They were from the house that Jimmy and I broke into and they were out looking for blood!

My heart sank and I knew I was in big trouble. Jimmy no longer lived at the foster home so I was taking the fall for the whole deal.

Apparently the owners of that house we had broken into looked all over town for the culprits. They found the dealer that we got the marijuana from with all that loose change. The jig was up.

The dealer was a friend of mine and knew where I lived. He had no choice but to give me up. These were hard-hitting men, the Blackwell brothers, leaders of a hillbilly mafia in the area! They pressed him very hard for the information and eventually he gave in.

Terri told me that a few of the guys from that group were coming over to talk to me the next night so I couldn't leave. Sure enough, the next evening two men from the group showed up and sat with us in the living room. They appeared to be non-threatening and they held a calm composure that made me very nervous.

They asked for the jewelry back so I gave it to them. They proceeded to give me a pep talk, telling me that all would be forgiven if I went over to the house and mowed their lawn once a week. They also told me that if I got lazy while performing that duty there would be people there at the house who could motivate me.

I knew what was up. They just wanted to get me over to their house so that they could deal with me their way. I was really scared at the thought, so in the middle of the night I snuck out of the house and ran away. I would go to my grandparents in Kelowna, where my brother happened to be living at the time.

That night I walked twenty kilometers (twelve miles) to Vedder, just outside of Chilliwack, where one of my break-and-enter partners Chris lived. I told him all about the jam I was in, emphasizing the part about the Blackwell's chasing me down, and that I had to get out of the area and make a run for it!

Chris gave me some money that he got from a score, which I used to take the Greyhound bus to Agassiz. I would have to break into a house in Agassiz to get the money to pay for the rest of the trip to Kelowna.

Once I arrived in Agassiz, I broke into a few houses but there was no money to be found. When evening came, I went into a public washroom and laid down on the lengthy sink countertop and went to sleep.

**Into The Dawn**

I was awakened abruptly when an evil spirit began to pull at my hair! I was under a vicious attack from this dark spirit and I felt intense pain from a burning sensation on my head! It also felt like he was biting me!

It took all I had to get out of there and run across a field trying to escape this act of violence! About halfway across the field the spiritual assault subsided and I walked the rest of the way across trying to recover.

I walked towards a public community center and noticed that there was a back door that was wide open. I went to the door and listened to see if anyone was in there. I didn't hear anything so I went in. It was empty, much to my relief.

I had a look around and in one of the closets in the back room I found a coffee can that was used for donations. There was $26 worth of loose change in the can, which meant I could take the bus the next day.

I found another room where council members from the town had board meetings in, so I sat in one of the chairs, laid my head on the lengthy varnished oak table and went to sleep.

When morning came I walked to the Greyhound station and it turned out that I only had enough money to make it to Penticton, Ninety six kilometers (sixty miles) from Kelowna. I bought a ticket and boarded the next bus.

When I arrived in Penticton about six hours later I knew I would have to hitch-hike the rest of the way to Kelowna. I walked from the bus terminal to the highway and stuck out my thumb.

**Eric Badke**

About a half hour later a lady picked me up her convertible. It had the top down. After I got in, she told me she was also going to Kelowna. As she drove we listened to Van Halen on eight-track tape and the sensation of having the cool wind blow through my hair was pleasant.

When we arrived in Kelowna, she dropped me off at a corner store, I thanked her for the ride and she drove away. I used a pay phone to call my grandparents so they could pick me up. Roland came on the line and told me that my social worker called earlier and told my grandparents that I ran away and that I would probably show up there.

I stayed a few days with my grandparents and my brother, but I had to leave. My social worker had a new foster home for me in Abbotsford.

# Chapter 14

Not long after I moved to Abbotsford I got a job picking raspberries on one of the many farms in the area. About three weeks later, my foster mom came to where I was picking berries to tell me that someone wanted to talk to me. I was curious so I left raspberry rows and went down the dirt road to the main house.

My heart sunk in my chest when I saw a police officer standing outside his car waiting for me. As I approached him he asked me if I was Eric Badke and I confirmed that I was.

He said, "Eric Badke you are under arrest for four counts of break and enter."

He read me my rights and then asked me to put my hands behind my back. He clasped the handcuffs onto my wrists and placed me in the back of his cruiser. He told me that he was taking me to the Chilliwack detachment where I would be questioned and placed in cells to await court in the morning.

On the trip to Chilliwack my mind was swimming with confusion. How did I get caught?

When we arrived at the detachment the police officer took me into booking, fingerprinted me, and took my photo. He then placed me in the cell and told me he would be back later to take me to another room to question me.

About a half-hour later he took me out of the cell and led me to a room where another officer was waiting for me. They proceeded to tell me that the rest of our group: Jimmy, Wally and Chris were also in custody. They told me that after Chris was caught doing a B&E, he informed on the rest of us in order to gain a lighter sentence.

It was no longer a mystery as to how I got caught. I was informed on and that made my blood boil. Apparently there is no honor among thieves after all! All I could think about was what I would do if I got my hands on Chris!

The officers asked me if I wanted to give a statement so I did. I confessed to my crimes. What I didn't know at the time was that I should have spoken to a lawyer before giving a statement.

In the morning, I went to court and spoke with a court-appointed attorney. It was confirmed that I was being charged for four counts of break and enter. The case against me was clear cut due to my confession so my lawyer suggested it would be easier for me if I plead guilty. I agreed.

When I went before the judge I pleaded guilty and was released with a promise to appear in court at a later date for sentencing. My social worker drove me back to the foster home in Abbotsford. I was glad to be free from jail for the time being.

About a month later it was time to go to court for sentencing. I truly believed that my crimes weren't that serious and that after court I would be coming back home for lunch. I was dead wrong!

When my case was called and the prosecutor read the charges, the details of my crime, I kept my composure. After my attorney spoke in my defense it was time for the judge to go into his chambers to go over my case.

After the judge deliberated and came back into the courtroom the bailiff yelled out,

"All rise!"

When the judge sat down we followed suit. He peered at me over his glasses and told me to rise.

"Eric Badke, after much consideration and due to the seriousness of your crimes, I sentence you to twelve months open custody." He then slammed down the gavel and departed!

I was extremely shocked! What did this mean? I was shaking my head trying to process the ruling the judge meted out. I was undeniably not going home for lunch on that ill-fated day.

The sheriff came over to me, grabbed my arm and led me out of the courtroom. He led me to the back of courthouse to where the cells were and proceeded to lock me in. I sat there for three hours in confusion, still trying to comprehend what had just happened to me.

The year was 1989, I was seventeen, and I was going to be in prison for a whole year! That was a long time!

**Eric Badke**

# Chapter 15

At around 3:30 that afternoon I was taken to city cells at the police detachment. At dinnertime we were served take-out Chinese food and it was a rare pleasure all things considered.

Being behind bars overnight was a different experience altogether. The mat was hard, I had no pillow, I was monitored by camera, and the light was kept on all night. I had a hard time sleeping.

After they served breakfast the following morning I was informed by the guard that they were transferring me to the Youth Detention Center (YDC) in Burnaby. I was placed in handcuffs, led to a Sheriff's van, and positioned within the cage in the back.

It was good to be out of the cell and on the road even though I was traveling towards an unforeseeable future. I had no clue what was in store for me.

After we arrived at YDC I was led to booking, was given prison-issue clothing along with a pouch of tobacco, rolling papers, and toiletries. I found out that there were two sections to the detention center: closed custody and open custody.

Closed custody had a unit system that held the more hardened criminals, including teens that had committed murder, armed robbery or rape, for example.

Open custody (Holly's Cottage), was a more relaxed system where we weren't locked in our rooms at night and we were able to go into the yard and exercise most evenings. The entire compound was surrounded by a high fence topped with razor wire.

I was placed into Holly's Cottage and I stayed there for about ten days. While I was there I had a roommate that had the same charges I had: four counts of B&E. He only received three weeks. It didn't seem fair! Later on I found out that the judge that sentenced me (being a victim of B&E himself) was widely-known in Chilliwack as "The Hanging Judge"!

After about ten days at Holly's Cottage I was notified that I would be transferred once again to another facility. I was going to be a resident of the Center Creek Detention Center. Center Creek was a work camp located sixty-five kilometers (forty miles) into the wilderness and was about sixteen kilometers (ten miles) short of Chilliwack Lake. It housed around thirty-six inmates and was an open custody institution.

So once again I was shackled and placed within a van. I was among other inmates who were also being transferred to Center Creek. We all shared one thing in common: we had no idea what was in store for us and what to expect at this new facility.

Once we arrived at the camp we were unshackled, led into the office, and booked. We were then issued work clothing (greens), steel toed work boots, casual clothing, and shoes. We were also each given a towel, toiletries and a pouch of tobacco with rolling papers.

This camp consisted of a main office building, six cabins that housed six inmates each (including an honor-unit for residents who deserved extra privileges), a dining hall with a restaurant style kitchen, a recreation hut that had pool tables, a workout room where we could lift weights, a laundry room, a gymnasium where we could play floor hockey, a soccer field, a baseball diamond, a fish hatchery building in proximity to the creek, a school portable, an automotive shop, a wood shop, and a tool shed.

After we were given our prison issues we were assigned a cabin. I would be placed within cabin three that had an open concept design. I was sort of nervous once I was set loose to enter the camp. I sat on my bed in the cabin and when the lunch horn went off I went to the dining hall.

What I didn't know at the time was that I would be walking into a vipers nest!

When I entered into the noisy dining hall I observed that there were six large picnic style wooden tables with six inmates sitting at each one. I sat down at cabin three's table and I surveyed the scene. These prisoners all looked very menacing indeed! A lot of them had long hair and a strong build.

I became aware that one of the three guys from my B&E crew was sitting at cabin two's table. It was Wally! He was here! I couldn't believe my eyes!

One of the inmates from cabin four's table called out to Wally,

"Hall! Is that him?" he pointed to me.

Wally nodded his head in confirmation. That inmate, whose name was Powchuck, one of the "heavy's" of the camp, pointed and called over to me,

"Are you Badke?" (In prison we are always called by our last name)

I nodded nervously.

"You broke into the Blackwell house! You're dead!"

How did he know that? Wait a minute…what treachery! In order to gain status at the camp Wally told the heavy's what I had done!

After Powchuck informed me that I was "dead" most of the inmates stopped talking, turned their heads, and eyeballed me. At that moment all I wanted to do was shrivel up and disappear. My throat gulped, my face turned red with embarrassment, and my heart sunk. After I received the threat I felt much fear and anxiety towards what was going to happen to me after lunch. I now wished I had never broken into those houses that got me here.

After lunch a couple of heavy's named Dodge and Easton stopped me on the front porch of the kitchen and began to play mind games with me. There were no guards around.

Dodge, who was the Alpha male of the camp, told me that everyone was going to take me and lynch me from a tree.

He then took a swing at me but stopped short before he made contact. It made me flinch.

### Eric Badke

"Two for flinching!" He shouted and smiled. He then subsequently punched me very hard twice in the shoulder. The impact was extreme but no matter what I couldn't display the pain. This "two for flinching" game would be an ongoing ritual during most of my stay at Center Creek.

Another camp dweller came out of the kitchen. His name was Lounsberry and he was from Chilliwack.

"So you're the dude who broke into Blackwell's? You have a lot of balls! Do you have any idea who they are and what they are going to do to you? Do you have a smoke?"

I reached into my pocket and produced the pouch of tobacco that I was previously issued. Lounsberry quickly snatched it out of my hand and began to walk away.

"Hey screw you! Give that back!" I yelled. Big mistake!

Lounsberry then turned around, advanced toward me, and got right in my face. His nose was about an inch from mine and he was scanning my eyes with his.

"Do you have a problem? We could settle this right now or how about later?" he sneered.

He was very self-confident and I was daunted to say the least. Half the camp was watching.

"No I don't have a problem." I replied sheepishly.

**Into The Dawn**

He then spit in my face and walked away! I couldn't believe it! I have never been so insulted! I did the best I could to wipe the spit from my face onto my sleeve.

Easton then walked up to me and informed me,

"You are going to be one hurting dude later. You should go into PC."

PC meant Protective Custody. If one went into PC that meant that one would be transferred into another facility that contained protected inmates who were rats (informers) and skinners (rapists). If one went into protective custody it was one of the lowest forms of status an inmate could ever have. If you were labeled as a PC you could become a target for those on the street after you got out of prison. That was the last thing I was going to do.

Easton then took a swing at me and I flinched.

"Two for flinching!"

He proceeded to give me two hard ones to the arm right on top of the newly formed contusions that Dodge had just provided me!

I turned and walked away towards my cabin. A barrage of insults was being hurled at me from the other convicts who were standing outside of the dining hall. It was not my proudest moment to say the least!

What I found out later was that the administration of the camp would periodically check residents for bruises every couple of days. If anyone showed up with bruises on their face the whole camp would be disciplined and lose privileges. If anyone was caught assaulting another resident or fighting he (or they) would be sent on disciplinary leave for two weeks of closed custody at YDC in Burnaby. These were policies that would diminish the punishment that I would receive from the other convicts but they would find other ways to mistreat me.

The inmates would occasionally spit in my face, they would kick me painfully in the shins with their steel toed boots, throw rocks and sticks at me while out on work detail in the bush, and would continue to torment me psychologically and verbally.

I only made a few friends at Center Creek. Most of them were going through the same abuse that I was. We were a minority.

Before I came to jail I thought I was street smart and cool but I had nothing on these heavy's. They were very intelligent, probably demon possessed, and most of them were gang members. They had a strong desire to prove themselves to their friends and gain status within their gang.

One day I decided that enough was enough. While I was attending school in the portable one of the inmates, whose name Burns, took my pen and wouldn't give it back. I got aggravated and I grabbed him by the neck. I told him that I would fight him after school.

After I let go of his neck and turned around he one-punched me with a right hook from behind and got me in the jaw! I was knocked out cold and I fell to the floor unconscious.

When I awoke one of the guards, who was summoned because of the incident, helped me to my feet. I didn't know where I was and I couldn't remember what happened or why I was on the floor. As the guard was leading me by my arm toward the cells located in the main office building I was confused and I continued to question,

"What happened?"

He wouldn't answer me which added to my vexation. It wasn't until after I had been in the cell for about an hour that my memory came back to me. Burns had knocked me out!

Oh how I wanted revenge in the worst way!

I, along with Burns, was transferred to YDC (closed custody) for two weeks disciplinary. We were placed within separate units. I will spare you the details of my stay in unit one. It wasn't good and I saw things I would rather not repeat.

About a week after I was returned to Center Creek, Lounsberry went on a pass to go to his home in Chilliwack for three days. While he was out he contacted the Blackwell's and told them that the guy who broke into their house was at Center Creek.

He got the green light from them to take care of some unfinished business with me when he got back to camp.

After Lounsberry returned to camp he informed me about what the Blackwell's had conveyed. What he articulated made me very tense and uneasy. My adversaries at the camp would now wait for an opportune time to take care of me. That prospect presented itself a couple of weeks later.

Right out of the blue the guards at Center Creek decided to go on strike. They cleared out of the compound and began to picket down by the front gate one hundred yards away from the camp.

A limited amount of uniformed police officers were brought in but they didn't patrol the interior or perimeter of the camp. They stayed in the main office and observed us from the front window. They were "police officers" not experienced "corrections officers" so they were out of their element during the strike.

Earlier I was on the porch of the dining hall having a 4 pm coffee break when I observed a resident come out of the office. He announced to a few heavy's that just got off work detail and were now hanging out outside of cabin one,

"The guards are on strike!"

Easton was there and he declared,

"Let's get Badke!"

They all agreed and began advancing towards my cabin when one of them recalled and called out,

"He's working in the kitchen!"

"We'll get him afterwards!" Easton proclaimed.

**Into The Dawn**

I couldn't believe they didn't see me viewing them from across the compound! I quickly turned and retreated into the kitchen. My heart sunk with foreboding realizing that I was going to be one hurting dude later.

After my break I assisted the head chef with preparing dinner knowing that I was going to take a beating after my shift. I told myself that I have to be brave and did my best to psych myself up for the inevitable.

When it came time for the camp dwellers to come in and line up for dinner I was positioned behind the counter dressed in my kitchen-whites serving. As I distributed the food, one by one the residents would glance at me with a menacing and knowing smile. Some of them would gaze at me in the eye and shake their heads in pity as if to give me the implication,

"I am glad I am not you!"

I did my best to put on a brave front. I couldn't display my fear so I continued on business as usual.

**Eric Badke**

# Chapter 16

After dinner I set off to my cabin. Easton was standing there smoking a cigarette waiting for me. He gave me an ultimatum,

"Well Badke here's the deal: you can either take a beating or you can AWOL."

AWOL (Absent With Out Leave) meant that I would have to escape from the camp, scramble sixty-five kilometers (forty miles) through the bush towards Chilliwack, and risk being chased down by dogs. They would seize me and it would be an automatic nine months added onto my sentence.

I decided I would take my chances out in the woods. I didn't want to catch a beating. I informed him,

"I will AWOL."

He smiled, nodded his head, and slapped me on the shoulder,

"Good choice Badke! Get going."

He then pressed the cherry of his cigarette onto my cheek, turned and ambled away.

I winced at my newly developed throbbing burn wound. I was in a world of hurt! I exhaled, turned, and strode into my cabin.

"I'm going to do this!" I whispered pumping myself up.

I changed my clothing, tucked my pants into my socks, and made one last trip to the bathroom. When I got out of the bathroom I realized that my plans to AWOL were being interrupted by an unexpected intrusion.

Lounsberry and another hoodlum named Kale were standing in the common area of the cabin waiting for me. Lounsberry uttered,

"Fight back Badke, make this interesting for us!"

And so began the two hour gauntlet of turmoil. I would embrace the chaos as convicts would come into my cabin and take turns assaulting me. They mostly gave me body shots. I let them have their way with me and didn't fight back. Even though I pretended that it did, after a while it didn't even hurt anymore. A couple of hours later they stopped coming into my cabin much to my relief.

After the beatings subsided I took the opportunity to leave the cabin to enter the safety of the compound. I staggered into the open area and sat at a picnic table outside of cabin three. Dodge, who had massive muscles and was the main heavy of the camp, came out of the cabin and positioned himself next to me.

"So it looks like you've had a rough time of it Badke. I have tobacco in my cabin why don't you go in and roll yourself a smoke?"

"No that's okay" I told him.

"No go ahead Badke, go roll yourself a smoke" He nudged me from behind towards the cabin.

I reluctantly decided that I would do as he said. I warily entered his cabin located his tobacco, and began rolling a smoke. A half way through making the cigarette Dodge came into the cabin with glaring eyes and a smile on his lips.

He took a swing at me and stopped short. I flinched.

"Two for flinching!" he announced.

I expected two to the arm but Dodge had something more sinister in mind. He wound up but his punch didn't go to my arm; he smashed me right in the eye! The massive impact caused me to cry out in agony! I was bent over holding my eye and wailing! I had never been hit so hard in my life!

"Uh oh." Dodge uttered, feeling remorseful.

He probably believed that he really damaged me and in the worst way it felt like he did! All of a sudden Kale darted into the cabin, grabbed me by the shoulders, and began to knee me in the stomach.

Dodge spoke, "Leave him alone Kale, I think he's learned his lesson."

"Oh okay." Kale answered obediently.

As I turned to walk out of the cabin Kale unexpectedly gave me one last hard hook in the mouth with his right foot from behind. I whimpered from the shock of it and strode out of the cabin. My gums were now bleeding.

After I went back to my cabin and I had a look in the mirror. My eye was tremendously swollen shut and the eye itself was throbbing. It was excruciating when I moved it. I am surprised Dodge didn't break the orbital

**Into The Dawn**

bone that surrounded my eye! I now had to go display my shiner and burnt cheek in the dining hall while serving evening snack.

Once I took my beats things began to mellow out for me at the camp. I was now under Dodge's protection as he told all the heavy's to lay off me. I gained a bit of respect from the camp dwellers because I didn't go into PC and I didn't rat. I also survived a punch in the face from Dodge which within their eyes was epic!

Following the staff strike I was moved into cabin five which was the honor-unit. Cabin five received extra privileges that other residents didn't receive. I now had a room with a door, a comfortable bed, access to a pool table, a washer and dryer; a living room that had couches, satellite TV, and stereo. In the dining hall our table was always called up first to line up for the meal.

On Friday evenings we would have an extra privilege: a guard would take us in a van to go to a movie in town, which was nice if we wanted to spend the money.

I began lifting weights, took up boxing, learned how to punch, and when I got into fights I began to win! I was no longer considered a pushover by the other heavy's in the camp because they knew that I now had no fear and would fight back.

Even though I was incarcerated there were good things about being at Center Creek. I learned how to play guitar, read some good books, got an education, played floor hockey, went mountain biking, went on a group outing to go downhill skiing at Manning Park, a group of us went up in a plane and flew over the Fraser

Valley, and my Dad and brother would come visit on the weekends periodically bringing me food from McDonalds.

**Roland visiting me at Center Creek,1989.**

Although these were good experiences I longed for my freedom. Time went by at a snail's pace. Each day felt like a week, each week felt like a month, and each month felt like a year. I remember having a coffee break outside of the dining hall after being imprisoned for seven months thinking,

"Wow I have five more months of this!"

It wasn't a good feeling but I had to make the best of it or else I would have gone insane.

## Chapter 17

After being at Center Creek for ten months I was given an early release for good behavior. I had money saved up which was good. One of the guards drove me to the Greyhound, dropped me off, and that was it! I was finally free!

My brother was living in a foster home in Hope BC so that's where I decided I would go. I bought a ticket and got on the bus. About a half an hour later I reached my destination and I was excited that I was going to see my brother again. He told me earlier on the phone that he would meet me in the park so that's where I went.

Roland was in the park sitting at a picnic table with another youth named Mike. Mike was also living at the same foster home that Roland was.

It was awesome to see my brother again and the first order of business was to get some beer. We went to the liquor store and found someone to bootleg for us. After we obtained the beer from the bootlegger we thanked him then went down to the Coquihalla River to drink and socialize.

It was a nice sunny day and before long we had a nice buzz going. It was so good to be free from jail after spending so much time there. I couldn't believe it! Not being monitored by guards and harassed by other prisoners was something that I had to get used to.

After we depleted the beer we began walking to the foster home. I was allowed to stay there a couple of nights while I got my affairs in order.

**Eric Badke**

A couple of days later I received a check from welfare and I paid for a room for the month at the Mount Hope Motel. I had $200 of support left over so I used that money to buy one hundred hits of acid from Vancouver. I could sell the acid for $10 a hit and make an $800 profit so that is what I did.

It didn't take long before most of the partiers in town knew that I had acid and they came to purchase it off me in droves. Having acid in town was very rare so it was a novelty now that I made it available. I met a lot of people and became quite popular to my new peers. My room at the Mount Hope Motel became the hot spot for youths within my age group to drop by, hang out, smoke weed, and drink alcohol.

It wasn't long before I got a job at the Rainbow Junction restaurant washing dishes and I began to attend night school. I moved from the Mount Hope Motel to an apartment that was above the pool hall/arcade. My new room-mate was a youth my age named Jay.

Anybody who was cool hung out at the pool hall and when they wanted to gather they would come upstairs to the apartment. We would host significant parties that would extend to all hours of the night.

Roland and I both had girlfriends. One Friday evening I was hanging out with my girlfriend and a large group of youths in front of the pool hall. My brother was about a block away on the side walk arguing with his girlfriend.

Out of nowhere a police cruiser quickly pull in front of my brother like gang busters and slammed on its brakes! Two police officers got out of the car abruptly and rushed at my brother! One of police officers grabbed my brother by the neck and pushed him behind a bush adjacent to the sidewalk. I observed his elbow coming up and down as he assaulted my brother! There was no cause for this action that I could see so I ran down the sidewalk towards this scene of upheaval being trailed by all my friends. When I arrived at the scene the other cop approached me with his hands outstretched.

"Stay out of this Badke!" He said.

"What are you doing to my brother?" I bellowed.

He replied, "Stay out of this Badke or I will place you under arrest!"

"For what?" I asked with agitation.

"Obstruction of justice!" he answered.

"Yeah right!" I hollered!

I tried to bypass him to assist my brother but he blocked me, spun me around, and put me in a choke hold! He dragged me over to the car and opened the back door. I felt myself passing out from the choke hold so I put my foot into the car indicating that I gave up. He released me, informed me that I was under arrest for obstruction of justice, placed me in the back seat of the cruiser, closed the door, and went to assist his partner who was still struggling with my brother on the pavement. My brother was fighting back with all he had. He proceeded to snap one of the officer's fingers.

**Eric Badke**

By now there was a large crowd gathered around witnessing the scene and yelling at the cops to leave us alone. It wasn't long before the officers had my brother in handcuffs and they placed him in the back seat of the cruiser beside me.

"What the heck is going on?" I yelled.

I couldn't believe the injustice of it all! This was police brutality as far as I could tell and anyone who was witnessing it would agree! I saw my girlfriend in the crowd very worried and crying. I waved to her and blew her a kiss to reassure her that I was okay.

The cops drove us to the detachment and placed us in the drunk tank. We weren't even drunk! About an hour later, much to our relief, they took us out of the drunk tank and placed us within a normal cell that had beds.

I found out later that the reason why the police officers attacked in the first place was because my brother was drinking a can of beer on the street. That didn't justify what they did but justice wasn't on our side that evening.

We had to stay in city cells from Friday evening until court on Tuesday morning. It was miserable! Roland was charged for public drinking, and because he broke the officer's finger he was also charged with assaulting a police officer. I was charged with obstruction of justice and causing a disturbance.

When Tuesday morning came around we were brought to the courthouse. When we were led in to go before the judge we noticed that a large group of our friends who witnessed the scene were in the courtroom to support us.

We were released on a promise to appear in court on a later date for trial. While in jail I missed two days of work which added to the inconvenience.

To make a long story short, justice didn't prevail even though there was police brutality involved. The police officers were never reprimanded even though many complaints were submitted by those who witnessed the event.

When the trial came we were found guilty of our charges. Roland received two months in jail and because I was found guilty of obstruction of justice and causing a disturbance I received six miserable weekends in city cells.

**Eric Badke**

## Chapter 18

After we served our time life went back to normal. Roland left foster care and moved in with Jay and me above the pool hall. We continued to party every night.

Roland and I both got a job working for the Youth Corps building wilderness trails for $7 an hour. It was a good job and it lasted six months. We were drug dealers on the side. I bought my first car and I also bought a Blue tick/Redbone hound pup from the owners of the pool hall. I named him Chemo and he was a very cute pup. I will tell you a couple of stories about him:

When Chemo became a full grown dog I taught him how to open a door. He would jump up on his hind legs and twist the knob with his front paws! I would let him out and when he was ready to enter he would let himself in. it was quite the novelty but there was only one problem: he would go to any random house in the neighborhood, open the front door, and intrude into their house wagging his tail.

One evening around suppertime our next door neighbors had just baked a roast and they were out in front of their house having a cigarette. They had the roast cooling on the counter top in their kitchen. Chemo, having a keen sense of smell, detected the roast, opened the back door, went in like a burglar, grabbed the roast off of the counter, and ran out the open front door past the owners of the house! He had the roast in his mouth and he was going to have himself a feast!

A few minutes later the neighbors were pounding on my door very upset to say the least. Chemo needed to be punished but he was nowhere to be found.

After a couple of years of living in Hope, Roland began to sell cocaine. He was very successful at it and he always had a wallet full of hundred dollar bills. By that time I was a couple years into an addiction to crack. I couldn't sell it because I would always end up getting high on my own supply and deplete the product.

The year was 1997 and I was twenty-five years old. The party life began to take its toll on me. After many years of drug and alcohol abuse it not only made me less intelligent it began to affect my appearance. I didn't like what I saw in the mirror. Girls were no longer attracted to me and when I would attend parties I wouldn't join in any conversations because I had a low self-image. Nobody cared about what I had to say anyway, I thought. Due to the many years of drug abuse I not only lost most of my personality, I didn't fit in.

Roland was the most popular in town and I was the least. I wasn't happy and I didn't even want to be alive anymore. I was deeply depressed, everyone knew it, but it wasn't important to them. I wasn't as important as I used to be and knowing that added to my misery.

One day I was especially in the depths of despair. I wanted to kill myself but I was too afraid of the possibility of going to hell. I went down to the river, sat

**Eric Badke**

at a picnic table, cupped my face in my hands, and began to cry. After sobbing for about twenty minutes I walked into the river up to my waist and began to bring water to my face to wash away the tears.

Afterwards I went to the bowling alley to use the pay phone. Still deep in anguish I placed a collect call to my parents. Because I still harbored bitterness toward them due to our past encounters when I was a teenager I hadn't spoken to them for many years. At the time they were living in Fort Macleod, Alberta. When I got my dad on the phone my mom picked up the other extension so she could talk to me as well. I began to cry and I yelled into the phone,

"Why did you even have me dad? I wish I was never born!"

"What's wrong Eric?" My dad asked with concern in his voice.

"I don't want to live anymore! My life is meaningless!" I yelled.

And with that I hung up the phone and began to weep even more. A few minutes later I called them back and they both answered the phone at once.

"What's wrong Eric?" My mom and dad asked again.

"I'm having a tough time dad." I answered.

"We're glad that you called back we were worried about you. Where are you?"

"I'm in Hope." I answered again.

**Into The Dawn**

"Do you want to come here and stay with us for a while? I could come get you." My dad offered with compassion in his voice.

"That would be nice." I agreed.

What my dad did next was remarkable! He drove 990 Kilometers (six hundred miles) for ten hours one way to come collect me and my dog. I was very grateful and as far as I was concerned my dad redeemed himself for all the times he had seemingly wronged me during my teens. We had a great time conversing together during the ten hour journey back to Fort Macleod.

I stayed with my parents for two weeks and it was exactly what I needed. It was very therapeutic. My dad, Chemo, and I would go for walks along the Old Man River. We would look for heart shaped stones to bring to mom as gifts, and whenever we came across deer Chemo would chase them.

One evening I was out behind the house with Chemo having a cigarette when a skunk showed up in front of us. Chemo, being the hound dog that he is, trotted over to the skunk, stuck his snout into its hind parts, and elevated the skunk's back end with his nose. Needless to say Chemo got sprayed right in the face! Before I could stop him he ran into the house and began to rub himself into the carpet!

I informed my dad what had happened. The nasty aroma of fresh skunk spray was overwhelmingly all around us! We loaded Chemo into the back of the truck, went to buy tomato juice from the store, and brought him to the river. Using the tomato juice we attempted to wash the pungent stench off of him. We did the best we could but after Chemo's bath he still had a faint "fragrance" emanating from him. This odor remained on him for three long months!

After my two week stay with my parents I decided it was time to go back to Hope. My dad was very nice as he drove us home. Altogether my dad spent forty hours traveling 3960 kilometers (2400 miles) just for me because I needed him. I loved my dad for that! It was a very good experience and I was happy to be reconciled with my mom and dad after many years of separation.

**Into The Dawn**

## Chapter 19

After I got back to Hope I moved into a townhouse with Roland. I quit smoking crack but I began another addiction to prescription Tylenol 3. It was the euphoria and the pain killing effects from the codeine that had me hooked.

I decided that I wanted to get my life in order. I enrolled myself into the Hope Community College so I could acquire my grade twelve equivalency (GED). After six months of attending the college and preparing for the test I finally took it and passed. A couple of weeks later I received a certificate in the mail making the achievement of my grade twelve equivalency official. Roland wasn't impressed and I remember him asking,

"What good is having your GED? What is that going to get you?"

"Who says I am stopping there?" I responded.

Before the September semester came along I moved from Hope to Chilliwack to continue my education. The year was 1998 and I was twenty-six. In Chilliwack I attended the University of the Fraser Valley (UFV) and I began by upgrading math, biology, English, and computers.

After two semesters of upgrading I made an important decision. I decided that I would go for a Social Services Diploma. That would require a student loan. With assistance from student services I applied for the loan and I was eventually approved. It was advised by my career counselor that I should take all the electives for the Social Service Diploma before I entered into the program, so I determined to do just that.

When I began attending college my mind was below optimum performance from the many years of drug and alcohol abuse. Attending college was a struggle at first however after four years of studying every day my mind became strong, sharp, and developed. I also regained my personality and attractive facial features. I enjoyed attending college, I made some friends, I was gaining an education, and I had high hopes for a successful future in a career that I would enjoy.

Two years into my college education, in the year 2000 at age twenty-eight, I met someone online. Her name was Stacy, she was twenty-seven, and was a legal secretary from Toronto. We began to relate to each other via online chatting and after a couple of weeks she gave me her phone number.

I began to call her and we would talk to each other on the phone every night. When I called her at 6pm it would be 9pm in Toronto because of the three hour time difference.

We had so much to talk about and we got along great! I was very attracted to her photo (she had beautiful elegant eyes, and radiant red shoulder length hair) and I was dazzled by her personality, and her voice. After three weeks of conversing on the phone I was quite happy and I knew that I had already fallen in love so I revealed my feelings to her. She reciprocated by telling me that she loved me as well. I was electrified by her response! She agreed to become my girlfriend much to

**Into The Dawn**

my delight. The only problem was that we were 4350 kilometers (2700 miles) apart.

One evening I was visiting Roland in Hope when I told him about Stacy. While sitting at the dining room table with my brother I decided to call her. Stacy and I talked for a few minutes and Roland was listening to the way I was talking to her. He knew from the tone of my voice that I was in love with her. He told me to put her on hold for a minute.

"How would you like to go see Stacy in Toronto?" he asked.

"How?" I asked back.

"I will pay for it", he answered.

"Really?" I wanted to confirm what he was telling me. I could hardly believe that there was a possibility that I would go see Stacy in Toronto!

He confirmed it. I then took Stacy off hold and spoke to her,

"I have a surprise for you Stacy. My brother said that he would pay my way to come see you in Toronto!"

"What? Really?" She inquired. She was thrilled!

"Are you really coming to see me?"

"Yes Stacy I am coming to see you!" I responded. I was enchanted!

# Chapter 20

It was settled that I was going to Ontario so I began to make the arrangements. I would take the Greyhound there and I would fly back. I decided that I wanted to take the Greyhound to Toronto because I wanted to experience all the beauty that Canada had to offer. It would be a seventy hour trip on the bus from Chilliwack to Toronto and a four hour flight back. I would spend five brilliant days with Stacy after I arrived. We were both very enthusiastic that we were finally going to meet!

So the evening of my departure my friends drove me to the Greyhound terminal in Chilliwack and I boarded the bus. After traveling a couple of hours I went to sleep for the night. When I awoke early in the morning we were stopped at the Greyhound terminal in Banff Alberta. Banff is a small ski town in the midst of the Rocky Mountains.

It was a crisp sunny morning and the view of the pristine, peaceful, and immense snowcapped Rocky Mountains was breathtaking! We were surrounded with them! I felt quite blessed to witness such splendor!

After we departed Banff we continued on our journey eastward.

That evening as we traveled through the plains of Saskatchewan I beheld something very majestic in the night sky above us. A display of emerald green northern lights covered the whole expanse of the big prairie sky and was in full motion as it danced across the atmosphere. I was entranced by the appearance of this mystical presentation that was displayed above me! I had witnessed northern lights before but never was it anything compared to this! I felt very fortunate indeed to witness such a captivating event and it was seemingly a gift that was meant just for me. My thoughts went to Stacy and I wished she was with me to witness this. I am sure she would have loved it!

As we spent many hours traveling through Manitoba and Northern Ontario I enjoyed the scenery immensely. The beauty of it all was breathtaking! I especially loved Northern Ontario with its many lakes, pristine forested landscapes, and the innumerable amount of trees with its variety of different colored leaves.

Eventually after seventy long hours of traveling, the bus pulled into the Toronto terminal. I was very captivated by this fascinating city that I had just arrived in.

Once I dismounted the bus I looked for Stacy in the terminal. I spotted her waiting in one of the chairs reading a magazine. Once she saw me she smiled, closed her magazine, and ran over to hug and kiss me! It was magnificent to finally to be joined with the girl that I loved the most!

We caught a taxi, cuddled up, chatted, and traveled through the stream of traffic toward her apartment. The sidewalks were active with people going to and fro as the skyscrapers towered before us and extended up into the sky!

Stacy lived on Yonge Street which happened to be one of the main streets of Toronto. Once we arrived I was very awestruck by her one bedroom apartment. It had extravagant hard wood floors and marble walls. We sat down on the couch and had a glass of wine. She was a woman of substance way beyond my expectation; I was very impressed with her, and very much in love. As we talked it felt as though we'd known each other for a thousand years.

The following morning Stacy had to go to work. She left me a key because I wanted to leave the apartment and go out into the city, tour around, and shop for souvenirs. Once she kissed me goodbye and left for work I slept in for a bit then made myself some coffee, bacon, eggs, and toast for breakfast. It was a nice sunny day and I was very motivated to go out and explore the excitement of the city.

After breakfast I departed the apartment to hit the streets! Once I reached the downtown core of the city I began to go window shopping. There were many interesting shops to browse around in. Eventually I found a store that sold martial arts paraphernalia and went in. I looked around for a bit then decided to purchase a pair of practice numb-chucks and a couple of miniature black keychain butterfly knives. One would be for my brother and one would be for me. I knew that he would be happy with that.

Stacy had the following day off so we got into the car she borrowed from her parents and travelled the two hour trip to Niagara Falls. I could hardly believe how fortunate we were to go there and experience one of the amazing wonders of this world. As soon as we got out of the car I could hear the sound of crashing water against the rocks in the distance. As we got closer and closer to the Falls I was full of anticipation! Once we arrived at the view point of the Falls I was immediately riveted by how majestic they were.

*[The Horseshoe Falls lie mostly on the Canadian side and the American Falls entirely on the American side. Located on the Niagara River, which drains Lake Erie into Lake Ontario, the combined falls form the highest flow rate of any waterfall in the world, with a vertical drop of more than 165 feet (50 m). Horseshoe Falls is the most powerful waterfall in North America, as measured by vertical height and flow rate. The Niagara Falls is renowned both for their beauty and as a valuable source of hydroelectric power. (Wikipedia)]*

We viewed the falling water of the Niagara and took some photos. After lunch we toured around the main street and decided to visit the "Ripley's Believe It or Not" museum. It was an intriguing experience. We spent the afternoon doing touristy stuff as there was plenty to see. I bought a few t-shirts from one of the shops. To experience this wonderful day with the woman that I adored was beyond words. It was an astonishing day indeed! After our personal tour of Niagara Falls was concluded we had dinner at an Italian restaurant then drove back to her apartment in Toronto.

The next day we visited Canada's Wonderland, an amusement park. We spent our day experiencing the sixteen rollercoasters there. It was nice and sunny which was to our benefit. We managed to go on almost every roller coaster in the park. It was thrilling being strapped in and speeding down the track, going up, down, and upside down!

There was a variety of roller coasters and each one was fun in its own unique way. We were mostly in the seated position but on one of coasters we had our feet dangling and on another we were strapped in and standing up while going straight up, straight down, and through loops! We enjoyed it enormously and after we concluded our thrill rides we sat down and had foot long hot dogs, soft drinks and fries.

We were now within the cool of the evening so we appreciated sitting by one of the man-made waterfalls that was lit up with a variety of vibrant colors. Everything we saw that day was very pleasing to the eyes.

The next evening after Stacy got off work we went out for dinner with her friends then Stacy and I took the underground subway to go to the famous CN Tower.

*[The CN tower is a landmark in Toronto, over 553-metre tower featuring a glass floor & a revolving eatery with panoramic views. (Wikipedia)]*

Once we arrived we paid for the tickets and were led into an elevator that rose towards the uppermost section of the tower. It was a privilege that we were the only ones there at the time. After our thrilling ride up we arrived at the top and stepped out of the elevator. We had a panoramic view of the city and it was a very romantic occasion between the two of us. It felt as though we were on top of the world!

**Into The Dawn**

The following evening we had dinner with Stacy's parents, and I began to get nervous as we drove there. Once we arrived at her parent's apartment Stacy introduced me to her mom and dad. After hearing so much about me from Stacy they were pleased to finally meet me and I was delighted to meet them as well.

We sat down for a roast beef dinner that was accompanied by a glass of red wine. Our conversation was enjoyable and after dinner Stacy's mom cut my hair in the kitchen. It was nice to spend time with Stacy's family and once the evening concluded we said our goodbye's, left the car with them, and journeyed back to Stacy's dwelling by the subway.

The next day Stacy and I went to a nearby travel agency so I could buy a plane ticket home. After I purchased the ticket we bought some alcohol coolers and steaks for dinner. We had a barbeque out on her deck and listened to some music on her stereo. It would be my last evening in Toronto as I would have to travel back home that following day. It was the most romantic five days of my life and I was sad that I would have to leave my beautiful girlfriend the ensuing day.

Before Stacy went to work that Monday morning, she began to tear up and cry. I stroked her hair and tried my best to comfort her. We gave each other one final kiss and then she departed for work. I felt a melancholy within my heart that is hard to explain. I was going to miss her terribly.

During my flight back home I reflected on the magnificent week I spent with Stacy. It was a perfect experience in every way possible. I concluded within my heart that it would be remarkable if I could spend the rest of my life with her.

Once I arrived home I placed a call to Ontario. Stacy told me that my visit with her in Toronto was amazing and way beyond what she expected. She told me that she wanted to move to Vancouver the following spring to be closer to me. I was thrilled with her idea! Now we had something to look forward to. We both wished that we were still together but I knew that at least for the time being we could still speak together on the phone. It was the next best thing to being with her.

# Chapter 21

I continued attending college and I was at the point where I didn't need to take notes in class. Due to my mind being quite developed after many years of demanding study I remembered most of what was said during the lectures.

In English 101 class I composed a thirteen page research essay. The thesis was: Was Canada successful in assimilating the First Nations people? It was quite an undertaking and it took a couple of weeks to compile all the information and arrange it on paper. After completing and submitting the paper I ended up receiving an "A" and I was more than content with that. I was very proud of myself for what I had achieved.

After about four months of conversing with Stacy on the phone I began to sense that her demeanor began to change toward me. Fearing the worst I didn't want to bring it up but then I finally did. I asked her what was wrong and she told me that nothing was wrong. I asked her again and she eventually told me that she had fallen out of love with me the previous month. Our long distance relationship had taken a toll on her. After she fell out of love with me she was too afraid to hurt me by telling me so; while we had continued to talk on the phone she merely pretended to be in love with me. She told me that it would be our last phone call to each other and that our relationship was over.

I was shattered! My heart was broken! Before we hung up the phone I tried my best to reason with her but her mind was already made up. I couldn't believe it! So sudden! After we hung up the phone for the last time I wept bitterly. Stacy wasn't going to move to BC and I would never see her again. I had lost the love of my life and now I was out in the cold without her. I didn't know what to do as I was very confused. How did things go so wrong?

Missing her was the only thing on my mind for the longest time. I felt lost without her. I reasoned that it would have been better if she had died. The thing of it was that she still lived but had rejected me. The notion of that cut me to the core in the worst way. I knew I had to get over her but that was easier said than done.

**Into The Dawn**

## Chapter 22

Due to circumstances not in my favor I had to move from my apartment into a motel room. Once I had moved in I realized that there were fleas dwelling there from a previous tenant. Before I was able to exterminate them they had bitten me all over my body. I had sores everywhere, it was itchy, and my skin wouldn't heal. This just added to my torment.

Once January 2003 came along I received my student loan of $3,500. I moved out of that motel room and into a basement suite on the native reserve. I paid for my rent up until June and due to the dejection of losing Stacy I got back into using cocaine. I went on a week-long bender and I spent most of my student loan money on the drug.

Spending most of my money on the drug meant that I couldn't pay my college tuition so I had to quit attending classes. Because I would fail my classes by not attending them that meant I would forfeit any student loan money I would receive in the future. I was no longer a college student and my dreams at having a career as a social worker had come to crashing end. Perhaps I wasn't ready to become a social worker after all.

I didn't know what to do with my life so I began growing marijuana in the basement suite in the hopes that I would thrive and make a living out of it. I was still missing Stacy terribly every minute of the day, I was no longer a college student, I was once again hooked on crack cocaine, I had an addiction to codeine, and I had sores all over my body. The flea bites that I received from my previous dwelling had activated my eczema and it wouldn't heal. The extreme itchiness would have me up scratching half the night so most of my days were spent sleeping.

Roland was still a dealer of cocaine so he began to support me by giving me enough for one hit of crack every day. I would have to ride my bike a long distance every day to his apartment to pick it up and I lost weight in doing so.

At the time I was also heavily into shoplifting to supplement my crack addiction. I would also steal food in order to feed myself every day. I ended up getting caught by the store security. I was arrested and charged with theft. When I went to court I was found guilty and sentenced to an eight month period of probation. I had to meet with a probation officer every week and check in.

It was my probation officer that surmised that my problem was psychological so she decided that it would be for my benefit to attend counseling for an undetermined length of time.

Once I went I did derive some benefit from attending counseling twice a week. It turned out that I still harbored some anger towards my dad for the events that transpired between us during my teens. It was very good to get these events out in the open and address it. It was very therapeutic at the time but not a cure for the hopelessness that I felt deep within. I felt as though I wasn't getting anywhere in this world.

My life continued on like this for about eight months. I was still suffering from depression. I made a decision to get into Buddhist meditation to attempt to bring a trace of peace and balance into my life.

One afternoon I was especially miserable and still missing Stacy in the worst way. I was lying on my bed and crying. I decided to speak to God from my heart: "God my life isn't going very well. If you are there I need you to reveal yourself to me because I have never received any indication that you are real. I don't want to live a life of hell and then die and go to hell. What would be the profit in that? Please reveal yourself to me! I am ready!" With that I rolled over and went to sleep.

About three weeks later one night I was having a tough time falling asleep. It was about four in the morning and I was wide awake. I decided that I would turn on the TV and perhaps fall asleep while watching it. I went to go turn on the light but before I could, I felt something in the room. I couldn't put my finger on what it was but it felt tangible, pure, peaceful, blissful, and it seemed to fill the room.

"What is that?" I wondered looking around the room. I shrugged my shoulders and went and turned on the TV. Just as I turned on the TV an early morning Christian program was coming on. I then spoke: "Okay God you have my full attention. If you have anything to say to me through this program now is your chance to speak."

I watched the program and at the end of it the pastor who was previously preaching was now sitting behind a desk. He had a stack of letters in front of him that contained questions from new Christians about Christianity. He was going to attend to these questions.

The first question he addressed was, "Why should we fear God?"

Wow! This was a question that I had on my mind for many years! I thought that Christians were crazy because they would go around saying, "Fear God! The fear of the Lord is the beginning of wisdom".

I would think they were foolish because I believed that God was a God of unconditional love and a father figure; not an angry man in the sky with a big stick that wanted to punish us and that we needed to fear.

So the first question on the program was, "Why do we need to fear God?" I was very interested in what the television pastor had to say about that. After the pastor read the question he put the paper down and began to answer, "Fear is an ancient word derived from the word "revere" so when the Bible teaches that we need to fear God it is saying that we need to have a reverence toward God." Wow! I knew what "revere" meant! That meant "respect." "Respect" God! I could do that! I could respect God. Suddenly it all made sense to me and it brought relief to my soul. It felt as if a chain that had held me in bondage for many years had just been broken off from me.

**Into The Dawn**

The next question was, "If the Bible was written by God why didn't He include dinosaurs in the Bible? Because dinosaurs aren't in the Bible it is a strong indication that it was written by men and not God." This was another question that I had that was never addressed before! After the TV pastor read the question he placed the paper down, picked up his Bible, and said, "If you go to the book of Job the fortieth chapter verses 15 to 17 you can read about a dinosaur. He then turned to the book of Job and read out loud:

*"Look now at the behemoth, which I made along with you; He eats grass like an ox. See now, his strength is in his hips, and his power is in his stomach muscles, he moves his tail like a cedar..."*

The TV pastor put down his bible and asked us, his audience: "Now doesn't that sound like a dinosaur? He is a behemoth that eats grass like an ox and has a tail the size of a cedar and he moves it about." Once again wow! That sounded like a Brontosaurus! It felt as if another chain of bondage got released from me and fell to the floor. It was amazing. As he read through all the questions that newly developing Christians had sent in, all the doubts I had about the Christian faith were addressed. God had spoken directly to me through this pastor. All my chains of doubt and bondage had finally fallen away.

At the end of the program the TV pastor told us that if anyone wanted to give their heart to the Lord and become a Christian we should pray along with him. As he led us in the "sinner's prayer" I echoed it into my soul and that night I gave my heart to the Lord. For the first time in my life I felt a freedom that can't be explained in words!

*For it is the God who commanded light to shine out of darkness who has shone into our hearts to give the light of the knowledge of the glory of God in the face of Jesus Christ. (2 Corinthians 4:6)*

After the program concluded I lay down on my bed and went to sleep. The date was October 15, 2003, I was thirty-one years old, I was reborn, and I became a new creation in Christ.

## Chapter 23

The next day I rode my mountain bike to a pay phone in town to place a collect call to my grandparents. Once I got them both on the line we talked for about twenty minutes. Finally I revealed it to them,

"By the way, I gave my heart to the Lord last night and I am now a Christian!"

They could hardly believe it! They knew of my life circumstances over the years and had been praying for me that I would become a Christian and now it was a reality!

"Really? That's great!" They responded with joy.

"What do I do now?" I asked.

"You should get a Bible," They answered.

"I got one". I had found a nice leather-bound Bible in the garage earlier.

"And you should go to church," they continued.

I don't know about that I thought.

So we talked for about ten more minutes and then we concluded our conversation.

As I was riding my bike home I began to hear a voice speaking to me trying to plant doubts within my mind:

"Are you really a Christian? Are you crazy? Don't you know that you are going to lose all respect from your friends and you will become a loser?"

This voice kept talking to me until I arrived home. I went into my room, sat on my bed, and continued to doubt:

"Am I really a Christian? What do I do now?"

All of a sudden I could sense something with me in the room again! It was there again: that tangible peace, purity, and bliss that was there before in the earlier hours of the morning.

"What is that?" I wondered.

Then suddenly it was revealed to me: God was in the room. What? God was present in the room? Was it possible that the God of the universe was here with me at this very moment? Wow! No one had ever told me about this before! I had gone to the Baptist church with my grandparents when I was younger but I had never experienced anything like this! Was it possible? I determined that it was.

I felt a leading to grab my Bible, open to a random page, and read. I turned to the gospel of Luke Chapter 10 verse 27 which reads:

*"You shall love the Lord your God with all your heart, with all your soul, with all your strength, and with all of your mind, and your neighbor as yourself."*

I thought about this for a moment. Before I gave my heart to Jesus I was one who would sit down and meditate on Buddha in attempts at finding peace. Why not sit down and love the Lord my God with all my strength and with my entire mind?

So I got down into the meditation position and began to love God with all my strength. All of a sudden God's presence came into the room like a rushing wind and began to swirl around me. All I felt was ecstasy and a burning within my core that is almost impossible to explain. I was brought to a place that I'd never been before. God was in the room with me in an exceeding measure! My tears began to flow and I was doing my best to keep my composure as this experience was almost too overwhelming. I was enthralled as I couldn't believe this was happening to me. Needless to say this doesn't happen every day especially to someone like me!

After about twenty minutes the occurrence began to subside but I was still exhilarated! My face was wet with tears. I felt cleansed and purified. It was amazing! At the time I wondered if there was anyone else on earth that experienced what I had just experienced. Because He had encountered me in this way, for the first time in a long time I was very happy. I was full of appreciation and love toward my new Father in heaven.

The following day I slept in until noon. After I awoke I decided to do what I did the day before and open up the Bible to a random page to see what God had to tell me. I turned to Psalm 84:10 where King David wrote:

*"I would rather be a doorkeeper in the house of my God than to dwell in the tents of wickedness."*

**Eric Badke**

I considered this passage for a moment and looked around my basement suite. I had marijuana posters on the wall, crack and marijuana pipes, porno videos, and dirty magazines. It came to me that I was currently dwelling in a tent of wickedness and it didn't please God. The last thing that I wanted to do was displease my God so I grabbed a tarp, spread it out on the floor, placed all my wicked items onto the tarp, and then closed it up. I then proceeded to take it into the woods behind my house and bury it. I then went back to my basement suite, uprooted all my marijuana plants, gathered up all my grow equipment with the newly uprooted plants, and got rid of them.

I then went back to my basement suite and sat on my bed. I now concluded that my place was no longer a tent of wickedness and that God and I could now kick it together with no hindrances.

I decided to once again become unified with my God so I got down into the meditation pose to love Him with all my strength. Once again the presence of God came into the room like a rushing wind and I felt something like an invisible burning fire flood my entire innermost being. My tears once again began to flow. This was a precious experience that compared to none other.

After that at any time when I wanted to become unified with my God I would simply position myself to receive and he would come to join up with me every time!

It was after one of these "union with God" sessions that a voice came into my mind,

"You are the second coming of Christ!"

**Into The Dawn**

What? Could it be? Was God talking to me? Could I be the second coming of Christ? After I pondered this, and for a few minutes I foolishly believed it could be possible.

I then went to the Bible and opened up to the book of John. In the Bible wherever one finds red letters it is indicating that Jesus is speaking and teaching. I read a few verses. Jesus had a lot of profound things to say and I came to the conclusion that I wasn't Jesus. The intelligence involved with what Jesus was saying was way beyond me. I was nothing like Jesus! I then turned the page to John 7:45-46. These verses indicated a time when the opposition to Jesus from the religious officials of the day, the Pharisees, sent the temple guards to arrest Jesus but they came back empty handed:

*Then the officers came to the chief priests and Pharisees, who said to them, "Why have you not brought Him?" The officers answered, "No man ever spoke like this man!""*

I closed my Bible and concurred with what the temple officer had discovered about Jesus. I was not Jesus in the least. Thank God I had the Bible to set me straight! I then opened my Bible to a random page, picked a verse, and read from Isaiah 59:15 which states:

*"…he who departs from evil makes himself a prey."*

I closed my Bible and contemplated on the meaning of this verse. I had departed from evil that was for sure. Who had I become "prey" to? Then it came to me: the devil. Wow! Since I learned that God and His angels were real that meant that the devil and his demons were real as well! I was flabbergasted! What kind of world had I stepped into? Now that I was no longer a non-Christian with a blind mind (2 Corinthians 4:4) it meant that I had enemies to contend with and that demons were real! How can I protect myself? I had no clue but I somehow knew that if they killed my body they could never kill my spirit. That now belonged to Father God. I then came to another conclusion: heaven and hell were real. Amazing! It became clear to me that there was a heaven to gain and a hell to avoid.

That night I had dreams that included voices, demons, and hellfire. The demons had the whole night to mess with my mind. Around five in the morning I woke up and became frustrated. I decided to go upstairs. I took a chair and sat down by the sliding glass window that separated the interior of the house from the sundeck. It was still dark out but I determined to sit there until the sun came up. I had read in the Bible the previous day that Jesus was called "The bright and Morning Star" so I stayed sitting there in front of the window hoping that He would arrive with the morning sun.

The darkness of the night began to lighten up as the sun was doing its best to rise from behind Mount Cheam, a mountain overlooking Chilliwack (see front cover). The mountain was beginning to glow from behind and I began to anticipate a sunrise. It wasn't long before a small ray of sunshine began to glance out from behind the uppermost part of the rocky mountain peak. It shone out from above the summit of Mount Cheam and lit up the scattered clouds that were arrayed above the town. Soon the sun was completely up and I was relieved that the morning had finally arrived! I witnessed a beautiful sunrise that morning as the clouds were alight with a variety of different colors. A flock of seagulls flew by my window as if to say, "Good morning."

I was mesmerized! The demons were gone and I felt the relief of my Fathers presence cocooning me and protecting me. After watching the sunrise I got up from my chair and made myself some coffee and read a passage from my Bible. This would be a ritual that would continue with me every morning until I moved on from that place.

**Eric Badke**

# Chapter 24

*"By this we know the spirit of truth and the spirit of error." (1 John 4:6)*

When I had become a Christian I came to a decision that I didn't need to go to church. One Sunday morning though the demons, being full of the spirit of error were tormenting my mind by filling it with voices. They were doing their best to play off my pride telling me that I was a king more powerful than anyone else in the world. I had enough of their antics so I decided that I would need some help.

I got dressed, got on my bike, and went to the Chilliwack Native Pentecostal Church. Once I arrived I sat down at the front row of the congregation. I was eager to hear what the pastor had to say. The adversary was still attacking my mind!

After the sermon, the pastor asked if anyone wanted to come up for prayer. I jumped to my feet and was determined to be the first person up.

The pastor had a vial of anointing oil. He opened it up, put some on his finger, rubbed it against my forehead, then he placed his palm there. He then proceeded to pray in an unknown tongue. As he was doing this I felt like a cup that was being filled up. I saw what looked like a "black dot" departing from me and it flew away. The torment that I was previously experiencing within was now for the first time being replaced by the Baptism of the Holy Spirit.

No longer would the presence of God be all around me only. He would now be inside me filling me to capacity! That God sized void within me that I had previously tried to fill with the things of this world (drugs, sex, money, education etc.) was now filled with God's Holy Spirit. That afternoon I went home and had the most peaceful sleep that I had ever experienced before. The multitude of voices that were in my head was now gone for good.

*"...and the peace of God, which passes all understanding, will guard your hearts and minds through Christ Jesus." (Philippians 4:7)*

That evening I called my grandpa and asked him how to defend myself against the demons. He told me that I could command them to leave in Jesus name, that there was power in the name of Jesus, and that demons were subject to Him! He told me say to them,

*"The Lord rebukes you Satan!" (Jude 1:9)*

He told me that I could combat demons with scripture. He told me to look up 1 John 4:4,

*"You are of God, little children, and have overcome them, because He who is in you (God) is greater than he who is in the world (the devil)."*

He also told me to look up Ephesians 6:10-18

*The Whole Armor of God "Finally, my brethren, be strong in the Lord and in the power of His might. Put on the whole armor of God that you may be able to stand against the wiles of the devil. For we do not wrestle against flesh and blood, but against principalities, against powers, against the rulers of the darkness of this age, against spiritual hosts of wickedness in the heavenly places. Therefore take up the whole armor of God that you may be able to withstand in the evil day, and having done all, to stand. Stand therefore, having girded your waist with truth, having put on the breastplate of righteousness, and having shod your feet with the preparation of the gospel of peace; above all, taking the shield of faith with which you will be able to quench all the fiery darts of the wicked one. And take the helmet of salvation, and the sword of the Spirit, which is the word of God; praying always with all prayer and supplication in the Spirit, being watchful to this end with all perseverance and supplication for all the saints." (New King James Version)*

My grandpa continued to inform me that there are three things about the armor of God: we are given it at salvation, we need to grow into it, and we need to put it on every day. When we put on the armor we put on Christ. When the demons look at us with our armor on they see Christ and are repelled by Him.

My grandpa also told me that when we sin that we have to make it right with God through repentance. He explained that when we repent we turn 180 degrees away from our sin and back to God. He informed me that salvation is a road taken once but repentance is a road taken repeatedly. Nothing is more important than remaining in God's highest place where our continued repentance brings us.

So now I had a few things in my arsenal in order to come against the schemes of the devil.

### Into The Dawn

Over time I began to become quite a warrior in Christ but even though we are not to fear our enemy we need to be watchful of him because:

*"... our adversary the devil prowls around like a roaring lion, seeking whom he may devour." (1 Peter 5:8)*

I learned that we should not be preoccupied with the devil and his demons but we are not to dismiss them either. This world is at war, it is spiritual, and it is for our very souls. The devil wants to steal our faith, kill our commitment, and destroy our destiny. Jesus came to this world to transform our hearts and provide us with an abundant life! (John 10:10)

## Chapter 25

I had written previously that I had been attending counseling in order to overcome shoplifting and get a better grasp on life. Now that I was a Christian I had a different motive for going to the sessions: I wanted to share my Christian experience. During the next session with my councilor I began to talk to her about God and how He was talking to me through the Bible, other people, a voice speaking into my mind, and that He was guiding me. Due to my sudden transformation she looked at me and the expression on her face was one of worry. She then spoke to me,

"Well Eric, I believe that we have come to the end of this stage of counseling. I think we should take the next step and have you go and see a psychiatrist."

I had no problem with that. I concluded that I knew things that they didn't so I had a strong desire to reveal the truth to them. I made an appointment for the psychiatrist and within the following week I went to see him.

Once I was in his office and went through a few formalities, I revealed to him the same thing that I told my previous councilor: that God was real and He was talking to me. After about five minutes of sharing my Christian experience the Psychiatrist finally said,

"Could you wait here a few minutes while I go confer with my colleagues?"

I nodded my head and he left the office. I was quite pleased with myself that I was now spreading the truth about God.

Something that I forgot to mention was that since I was full of the Holy Spirit whenever opposing spirits of the demonic would come around me I could detect them. I would feel a pressure on my neck and have a strange taste in my mouth indicating a demon was in the room with me. It was then up to me to go into spiritual warfare in Jesus name in order to disperse the demon back to where it came from.

When the psych doctor came back into the room he brought a high-level demon in with him and I could sense it.

The doctor began to speak,

"Well Mr. Badke, I spoke to my colleagues and we came to a decision to admit you into the psychiatric ward of the hospital."

I couldn't believe what I had just heard.

"What do you mean? Why?" I inquired.

"Because God doesn't speak to people Eric, we are worried about you and we need to monitor you for a few days" he answered.

"Do I have a choice?" I asked.

"No, you don't." he indicated.

"I believe you are in the spirit of error here." I countered.

"Well we will see about that," he stated, "time to go." He motioned for me to go with him.

He led me out of the office and across the street to the hospital. My frame was vibrating as I felt the anti-christ spirit attacking me and causing me to become discouraged. It was a struggle just to keep my stability and composure. It was frustrating because I couldn't defend myself by going into spiritual warfare since the doctor was there with me.

The doctor led me up to the door and buzzed us in. He then he led me into a room and told me to sit. He informed me that a nurse would soon come and take me in. He also explained to me that he would be back in a few days to check up on me. Then he left the room, carefully closed the door, and quickly departed.

Once the doctor had departed I took the opportunity utter a quick warfare prayer under my breath. A few minutes later the intake nurse came into the room in order to take my information. I told her that I had just become a Christian and the reason that I was in the ward was because I told the psychiatrist that God was talking to me. I told her that I didn't believe that I should be in the psych ward whatsoever.

She nodded her head then revealed to me that she was also a Christian. This grabbed my full attention. She told me that God does talk to His people but those who are non-Christian do not have the capability to understand this truth. After she told me this I felt an assurance in my heart and it was nice to have her in my corner supporting me. At least she understood where I was coming from. I noted to myself that I would be careful about what I would say to a non-Christian in the future because they don't understand the things of the Spirit.

*But the natural man does not receive the things of the Spirit of God, for they are foolishness to him; nor can he know them, because they are spiritually discerned. (1 Corinthians 2:14)*

After she took my information she brought me to my room and then left me to get settled in. I decided that I would go use the phone to call the pastor who had given me his business card the Sunday previous. Once I got him on the line I told him my circumstance, where I was, and why. He asked me if I knew how to pray in tongues and I replied that I did. I had just begun to perform this type of prayer a few days prior to my entering the ward. He told me to go to my room and once again pray in tongues toward God.

After our conversation I hung up the phone and went to my room. I laid down on my bed and began to pray in tongues.

All of a sudden God's Holy Spirit came to me in a most extraordinary way! My cup was filling up and flowing over, it felt marvelous, and it was empowering! Now nothing else mattered except what was happening to me at that very moment and I became aware of boldness within that I had never experienced before!

About fifteen minutes later I got out of bed, departed the room, walked down to the common area, and sat down at a table where two other gentlemen were also sitting. I introduced myself to them and as the Holy Spirit burned within me I began to preach Jesus to them with boldness. I did the best I knew how for the new Christian that I was. They were very interested in what I had to say and before long other people that were in the common area began to gather around to listen as well. They were responding to what I had to say and were being drawn in by the Lord God Himself!

Later on in the evening I received a new room-mate. He was an elderly gentleman around sixty-five years old. His wife had recently passed on and he was in a state of depression missing her terribly. He had tried to take his own life by swallowing pills and was unsuccessful thanks to God.

**Into The Dawn**

I had a genuine concern and a strong desire to encourage him so I began to share my testimony about how Jesus changed my life, saved me, and brought me a peace beyond description deep within my soul. I spoke to this man for about two hours and after I was finished his countenance had changed for the better. I believe that the message that I shared with him may have inspired him to have a better outlook on life. I suppose that it is a possibility that a seed of hope might have been planted within his heart that very night.

The next day as I was once again praying tongues in a whisper, I heard someone outside of my door in the hallway praying as well. I went out to see who it was and it was a man who I had met earlier. I asked him if he wanted to have a talk with me in my room. He readily agreed and followed me into my area.

As we sat on the bed he revealed to me that he was a pastor but he felt as though he had lost his connection with God. He explained that something terrible had happened to him while he was on a mission's trip in South America and he had never recovered from it. I wouldn't pry so I didn't ask him what had happened that had affected him in such a way that would land him in the psych ward. Instead I asked him if I could pray for him and he replied that I could.

I asked him what he would like me to pray for and he requested that I would pray for him to receive the infilling of the Holy Spirit once again. I nodded my head, laid my hand on his shoulder, and began to pray in tongues. He had his eyes closed and his face was uplifted toward heaven. He began to rejoice as the Spirit began to fill him in a fresh and familiar way. After I completed the prayer he was now once again filled with the Holy Spirit, encouraged and smiling.

He got up off the bed and as I followed him out into the hallway he walked up to a nurse and told her that he was ready to go home. That very afternoon, after a meeting with his psychiatrist, he departed that place with a future and a hope placed within his heart. I was delighted for him and felt privileged to be a part of his recovery but all the glory goes to God and God alone.

After spending three days in the ward the psychiatrist that had admitted me showed up at my room. He asked me if I would follow him down to the main office so that we could have a talk. I agreed and began to follow him down the hall.

As we walked together I began to study him. He looked very unstable and agitated. It was as if the demon that was oppressing him was having an adverse reaction to the more powerful Spirit that was within me. I asked him if he was okay and he replied that he was.

"You don't look very good, I am worried about you." I told him.

He answered, "That is not what this relationship is about Mr. Badke. It's about you."

**Into The Dawn**

With that I shrugged my shoulders and followed him into the office and sat down with him.

"Well, Mr. Badke you have been here for three days and if you would like you can go home, but I advise you to stay a bit longer so we can assess you further."

"Nah, I have places to go and people to see," I answered.

I added, "You know doctor, what I told you about God speaking to me was true. I am an educated man and very objective. I used the scientific method to test my hypothesis and came up with the theory that God was talking to me. Just to add to that I want you to become aware that science is climbing up a mountain and when it gets to the top: theology will be there waiting for it."

"Well, we'll see about that." He answered.

He got up and shook my hand. He told me to wait there in the office for the nurse to come in and discharge me and then he proceeded out the door leaving me in the room alone. I felt very amused and victorious. God had taken what was meant for the devils evil and turned it around for His good! I was glad to have been used by God in order to reach people in the ward who were lost in their way. Seeds were planted; I trusted that other people would water those seeds, and that God would in His own special way provide the increase leading them into the renewing of their spirit and the salvation of their souls.

**Eric Badke**

I had a burning desire within me to take a part in leading lost souls to the Lord. The day after I was discharged from the psych ward I went to the library to go online. I was searching for evangelistic material so I could print it out and bring it back with me into the ward. Since anyone was allowed to go into the ward and visit with whomever they so desired I took the evangelistic material that I printed out and brought it in with me.

After I had arrived, I went out into the smoking area where there were men and women patients sitting around a large circular table. I took a seat and began to preach Jesus, how He had died for our sins, and that if they would ask for forgiveness and receive Him into their hearts by faith they would be saved and receive the gift of eternal life. I then passed out the material that I had printed out prior to my arrival at the ward. Those who were sitting at the table were eager to receive the material which brought me a measure of encouragement.

One of the ladies who was sitting across from me asked,

"How do you know that God is real?"

I told her, "I'll tell you what: If you give your heart to Jesus right here and now I will prove to you that He is real! Do you want to give your heart to the Lord?"

**Into The Dawn**

She nodded her head so I began to lead her in the sinner's prayer. As I lead her she sincerely asked God to forgive her of her sins and for Jesus to come and dwell in her heart. It was a very special moment for the both of us and perhaps for those who were also witnessing this event.

After she became a Christian I knew that she now belonged to God. I got up, walked over to her and stood beside her.

"I am now going to prove to you that God is real. Are you ready?" I asked.

She nodded her head with anticipation. I proceeded to lay a hand on her shoulder and I began to pray in tongues in order to magnify God. It took only a minute before I knew that she was completely filled with the Holy Spirit.

"How's that?" I asked.

"What did you do to me? You are a magic man!" Immediately I shook my head. "I've got to go call my mom!" she exclaimed overjoyed.

I explained to her that I wasn't a magic man and that everything that she had received was from God and God alone. She got some change out of her purse and ran to the payphone to place her call. When her mom answered the phone I heard the new-born Christian express,

**Eric Badke**

"Guess what mom I am a Christian now!"

I stood back and smiled. Finally my first convert for the Lord! I was very happy for her as she now had the Lord to take care of her and guide her along the way.

## Chapter 26

After I left the ward I went over to my brother's house. He was wondering why I hadn't been over to pick up my daily hit of crack within the past couple of weeks. I told him,

"I am a Christian now." I went on, "You know what Roland? Satan had been lying to us all of our lives and God is better than Satan!"

"So you think you're better than me?" he asked, agitated.

He proceeded to shove me out into the hallway of the apartment building then he slammed the door in my face. I stood there for a minute and then walked away. It was my first experience of persecution. It wouldn't be my last.

I spent the next three years drawing near to the Lord daily and learning about him from His word in the Bible. During my first year with the Lord on April 18, 2004, my brother's girlfriend gave birth to their son. I now had a nephew and they named him Zac. This just so happened to be Good Friday the day that I was baptized in the Vedder River.

After I was baptized on Good Friday April 18, 2004 I moved from Chilliwack to Abbotsford in order to attend the "Global Harvest" church. It was a popular charismatic non-denominational church and I felt privileged to become a member. They had a great worship band and they also preached the living word that would build me up and speak into my life for whatever circumstance I was going through.

God was amazing as He drew near to me every day although sometimes He would allow me to experience attacks from the enemy from time to time - sometimes daily. I believe that He allowed that to happen in order for me to become His warrior and gain spiritual muscle. For the most part though, God had me on His mountaintop so that I could be near Him and sense His presence with me every day.

After a period of time though I felt God's presence draw away from me. I couldn't understand what was happening, I was confused, and I believed that he was forsaking me even though He wasn't. I learned later that God allows us mountaintop experiences for a season to give us a taste of our destiny but after that we must spend a period of time within the reality of the valley wilderness. I was later taught that we learn things in the wilderness that one cannot learn on the mountaintop such as faith and perseverance that leads to spiritual maturity. Faith and perseverance are spiritual traits that set us apart and assist us in building our Christ-like character. Building within us a Christ-like character is a high priority with God. When one is in the valley they can go through long periods of time where they don't experience the presence of God. This is when one must live by faith. No one had taught me about this at the time when He seemingly first drew away from me so I was at a major disadvantage.

## Chapter 27

As I felt His presence dwindle away from me I went into a slight depression and became frustrated with God. I began to lose my appetite for Bible reading and attending church. It didn't happen overnight but slowly after being with Him for three years I drifted away from God. I moved back to Chilliwack and I eventually quit going to church.

I began to go over to my brother's apartment every night to drink beers and snort lines of cocaine. Roland was no longer with his girlfriend. After a couple of years Roland began to join me in smoking crack. Since he was now getting high on his own supply he lost his ability to sell it.

For Roland to be able to afford his apartment I moved in with him to help out with the rent. A couple of weeks after I moved in, due to Roland not paying the bill, our power to the apartment got cut off. For three months, during the winter, we had to use flashlights and candles in order to see at night. We had both reached our personal rock bottom as our quality of life was at an all-time low.

Just after the year 2009 arrived Roland decided to abandon the apartment and me to go to Kelowna and move in with a good friend that we knew from Hope. Abruptly, after my brother had departed, I found myself alone in a dreadful place where I no longer wanted to be. I felt lonely without my brother and I began to feel a panic within. I promptly left the empty messy apartment and walked to a phone booth to call my dad who was now living in Vernon BC.

When I got him on the line I asked him if I could come and stay with him for a while. After a bit of convincing my dad finally relented and agreed that I could come and stay with him and mom until I found my own place. He paid for my Greyhound bus ticket and the next day I boarded the bus that would take me 343 Kilometers (213 miles) to Vernon.

Once I arrived in Vernon my dad was waiting for me at the terminal. It was good to see him again. We drove to his house and he set me up in one of the spare bedrooms.

After about a week dad came to me and told me that it wasn't convenient having me at the house because they were in the process of trying to sell it. He told me that he had set it up so that I could stay at the Gateway homeless shelter that was located within the downtown core of Vernon. He told me that he would give me $100 so that I would have some comfort money while I settled there. I agreed, packed up my stuff, and had my dad drive me to the shelter.

I lodged at Gateway for a couple of weeks. I didn't mind it as it was a step up from the condition that I was living in while I resided in Chilliwack. After a couple of weeks at Gateway I was transferred to the "John Howard" another larger shelter that was in the outskirts of Vernon.

I began smoking marijuana every day with my new friends Matt and Rob. We got high in order to escape the mundane life we were faced with. Whenever I had enough money I would spend it foolishly on crack to try and benefit from its limited euphoric effects. Even though I hungered for that drug, after I used I was always left unsatisfied and disappointed.

After six months at the "John Howard" shelter I found a room in a boarding house. The rent was reasonable, it had a great downtown location, and it included free cable. My dad gave me a big screen TV so that was convenient for me at the time.

**Into The Dawn**

## Chapter 28

The year was 2009, I was 37 years old when one evening in October my life took a drastic turn for the better. I was watching TV as I did every night but this evening a program came on that changed everything. It was a documentary that featured on the 2012 Aztec prophesies. It was speculated that according to the Aztec calendar the world would come to an end at that time. The show had a major impact on me and after it was over I sat there contemplating it for a few minutes.

What if it was true that the world was going to end within a couple of years? What had I accomplished in life and what kind of legacy would I leave behind? I was living a selfish lifestyle that only created negative ripples in this world. This bothered me right to the very core of my being! Even if the world wasn't going to end in 2012 I still wanted my life to mean something. I had a desire within me to become a benefit not a hindrance to this world.

I came to the conclusion that I was weary of my lifestyle that was leading me nowhere. This was my spiritual awakening. I got down on my knees and asked the Lord to forgive me for abandoning Him for the years I had been away from Him. I asked Him to forgive my sins and come back into my heart. I desperately wanted to become a Christian once again and live the way He wanted me to live.

**Eric Badke**

As soon as I rededicated my life to the Lord He began to fill me once again with His Holy Spirit. I felt liberation within me that I hadn't experienced in three years. I went to bed with a smile on my face. I was determined that I was going to change and live a life in line with God's will. Now I had His Spirit to empower me to do just that.

The following morning I woke up with the presence of God still burning deep inside me. I could tell that He was happy that I was back in His world and I was excited that He was back within mine. I was so thankful towards my Father God in heaven who loved me very much and wanted nothing but the best for me.

It was a ritual of mine that when I woke up I would smoke marijuana and get high before I faced the day. I called it wake and bake. This morning was different though as I now had God with me. How could I get high now that I was filled with His Holy Spirit? It would be just like stepping into His throne room and lighting up. It was no longer appropriate for me to do such a thing of disregard. God was royalty and deserving of my full respect. I took my bag of weed and I was determined to flush it down the toilet. Just as I reached the door of my bedroom I heard an adversarial voice in my mind,

"Don't flush that. You are going to need that later."

I turned around, put my baggy down, and sat on my bed and reflected on this for a minute or two. I shook my head and grabbed my baggy once again and headed for the door and stood there for a moment. The voice spoke to me once again and told me it would be a mistake to flush it. I turned, placed my baggy down and sat on my bed. This struggle continued on for a while and around the fifth time that I went to the door it felt like an angel was holding me firmly in place so that I would go forward and not back. I shook my head. That was it! I went through the door, went into the bathroom, and dispensed my marijuana buds into the toilet. As I flushed it I observed as it swirled down and disappeared. I threw my empty baggy into the trash and went back to my bedroom.

As I sat on the bed I once again felt that old familiar feeling: the peace of God that only comes when one is in right standing with Him. I now had a new addiction. Matthew Henry once quoted: *Peace is such a precious jewel that I would give anything for it but truth!*

My landlord had come to me two weeks prior to my rededication to the Lord. He had given me notice that he needed me to move out. Every winter he had people come in from all over Canada to take up residence within the boarding house. They were ski bums who would come every year to ski the slopes of Silver Star: a world renowned resort within the mountainous outskirts of Vernon.

My monthly rent usually went direct to the landlord from Government Social Assistance. Once he had received the rent from them, a week before I had to move out, he gave me back the full amount of the rent along with my damage deposit. All together I now had $800 in my pocket.

Typically whenever I had money I would in desperation ride my bike as fast as I could to the phone booth to call my crack dealer. Now something was different: I had a supernatural self-control that only the Holy Spirit could provide. As far as the drugs were concerned my money would now stay in my pocket.

I decided to invest in a new wardrobe and a prepaid cell phone. The clothing that I had before was stolen so I bagged it up and donated it to the Salvation Army. The apparel that I now would be wearing would be legitimate and appropriate! I could tell that the devil was very displeased with me.

I also came to a decision that since I knew so many dealers in Vernon I would have to move away from the temptation. I went online and found a homeless shelter that was in Kamloops, a city that was an approximate two hour drive away. Because I knew God was looking after me I would go to Kamloops by faith. I had a full trust without reservation that I would get into that homeless shelter in Kamloops once I arrived.

**Into The Dawn**

## Chapter 29

It was October 30, 2009 that I moved from Vernon to Kamloops. My friends drove me and dropped me off with my luggage outside of the shelter. It was three in the afternoon an hour before the shelter opened. I sat there on the front steps of the building praying that the shelter wouldn't be full and I would get in. I had complete confidence and I wouldn't be disappointed.

When the shelter doors unlocked I went in and found out they had openings! They led me into the office, took my information, and then gave me the affirmation that I was now approved to remain in the shelter much to my relief. I now had a warm place to stay. I didn't have to sleep outside in the cold that evening much thanks to God and His favor being bestowed upon me during my time of desperate need.

Another reason that I wanted to move to Kamloops was that there was a special non-denominational church I knew about that I wanted to attend. I heard the pastor of that church (Nolan Clark) preach with passion and enthusiasm at a Todd Bentley Fresh Fire Ministries conference that was held in Abbotsford back in 2004. When Sunday came I found my way to the church and after I arrived I sat in a pew at the back of the congregation. It was remarkable that when the pastor came on stage he preached the living word and the message seemed to be directed right at me. He preached a complete summary of the Old Testament from the Bible bringing me back up to speed with what I learned before I wandered away from God.

After the service the church served a free lunch. I went up and got myself a plate of food and sat down with some men who looked very approachable. I introduced myself and shook hands with them. I told them that I was new to Kamloops and that I was currently staying in the men's shelter that was in town. I went on to tell them that I had been clean two weeks from using drugs.

One of the men sitting with us happened to be on staff at the "New Life Mission" residential recovery program that was located next door to the shelter I was staying at. He told me that I was qualified to enter that program since I had some clean time under my belt. All I needed was a referral from mental health.

The following day I went to the community mental health agency to get the referral that the mission required. Mental health told me that they no longer did referrals but that I had another option to go to the Indian Friendship Center and receive one from them.

Once I arrived at the center they informed me that they didn't give referrals until five days after one's first contact with them. They decided that they would make a special exception for me which was encouraging. I believed that this was the favor of God in full effect as I was receiving what I needed five days early which wasn't the custom as far as they were concerned.

I was very grateful after I received the referral that I required from the Indian Friendship Center. The following day I went to the New Life Mission in order to submit it. I spoke with the executive director of the mission and after we conversed for a few minutes in his office he decided to accept me into the program. Five days after I arrived in town I had entered the New Life Mission residential recovery program! I was blessed as this residence was a very comfortable place to settle.

It was a large building set up like a two story modern hotel. I was given my own room with key. The room, which was on the second floor, included a bed, a nightstand, closet, desk, and a couch. The bathroom was down the hall and when it was time to eat we had a restaurant style cafeteria on the first floor. We had an elevator that would bring us from the residential section on the second floor to the cafeteria which was on the first floor and to the laundry room that was in the basement. We also had a TV room and a computer lab on the second floor which was convenient. I felt very fortunate as God had supplied my every need as I knew He would.

I decided that I wanted to take the opportunity to learn as much as I could from studying the Bible. I knew that every word provided was the truth and had the power to transform my life and in turn, after learning scripture,

I could do my part to teach others. I had purchased a red Bible case with a zipper from a Christian book store for my New King James Version of the Bible. With my new sword at my disposal I was set. I decided to make the New Life Mission my personal greenhouse for spiritual growth so instead of watching TV in my spare time I would be at my desk every night studying the word of God.

**Into The Dawn**

## Chapter 30

After a month of attending the non-denominational church, I decided to try out a Youth Church that was located at the university in town. I would have to catch a downtown bus to get me there. I remember it was a very cold and stormy day as I set out towards town to catch the 9:30am bus. It was at least -10 and it wasn't very enjoyable walking outside during that storm but I was determined to catch the bus in order to check out the Youth Church I had heard so much about.

Once I arrived at the bus stop I stood and waited and waited but the bus didn't arrive. It was now ten minutes late and I, along with the fifteen other people waiting for the bus, were literally freezing to death. We all decided to abandon the bus stop and go wait for the bus inside the warmth of the Tim Horton's coffee shop that was nearby. The bus never came and I was furious!

"Why God did you allow this to happen to me?" I was asking Him within my mind. God was silent over the matter.

I decided that I would leave Tim Horton's and head for home. On the way I observed a church that was called the Vineyard. It seemed to be a good place to go inside, get warm, and attend the service so I went in. At least this Sunday morning wouldn't become a complete loss I thought to myself! They were just finishing up their worship music and once they concluded it they announced a ten minute coffee break.

As I advanced towards the coffee pot a friendly young man approached me and introduced himself as Randy. I shook his hand and gave him my name but I was in no mood for conversation so I left him and went for the coffee. While I was pouring a cup Randy showed up beside me again and I thought to myself,

"Oh no! Not him again!"

He inquired of me, "Eric I was wondering if you would like to attend a church home group on Tuesday night. We are focusing on the prophetic."

As soon as he told me that my mood completely changed. I was especially interested in attending that group which included other like-minded Christians. That is just what I had been looking for.

Immediately I became aware of why I missed that bus earlier. God had a better plan for me in mind. It is amazing how He has the ability to bring forth the good out of the bad! I told Randy that I was very interested in attending the church home group. He agreed to pick me up on Tuesday night so we exchanged phone numbers.

After the service I decided to make the Vineyard my home church and it would be convenient due to it being a couple of blocks away from my residence.

**Into The Dawn**

When Tuesday night came Randy picked me up to go to the home group. The owner of the home we traveled to and the leader of the group was also named Eric. He welcomed us in and we were soon joined by fifteen other Christians from the church.

We began by listening to worship songs. As a group we stood and held our hands up lifting a mighty praise to our God. After our magnificent worship session we listened to Eric speak on the prophetic. He then asked if anyone had received a word from God for anyone in the group. Words were spoken and I also received a word of prophesy from some of the people who were there attending the group.

I was informed that God was calling me to be a missionary to the First Nations people in Canada and beyond. It was very edifying as they spoke into my future and I received it with elation in my heart.

The next evening after dinner I ran into George, a friend of mine who I had met at the shelter in Vernon previous to my move to Kamloops. He was now staying at the Men's shelter where I dwelled before moving into the New Life Mission. He was one who would travel by faith from shelter to shelter so he could spread the word of God. Anyways, I asked him if he wanted to go to McDonalds for a coffee and he agreed to go. Once we arrived at the restaurant we purchased our coffees and then found a table in which to sit.

**Eric Badke**

I asked him if he wanted to do a bit of a study since we both had our Bibles with us. He agreed so we opened our books and began our study. About twenty minutes in we eventually began talking about Moses and the Israelites who had wandered the desert before entering the Promised Land. I was under the impression that they wandered the desert for eighty years but George was adamant that it was forty. We looked it up in the book of Exodus and sure enough it was forty.

A few minutes later a pretty young lady with very short dark hair came over to us and asked us what we were doing. We informed her that we were having a Bible study. She asked us if she could join us and listen in. We agreed and welcomed her to join us. She introduced herself as Stephanie.

After George and I introduced ourselves we discussed Moses and the Israelites for a few more minutes. Stephanie interrupted us by declaring,

"God would never forgive me."

"Why?" I asked her.

"Because I am a prostitute." She answered.

I thought about this for a moment then I asked her, "have you ever heard of Mary Magdalene?"

"Yes." she replied, "I used to be a Christian."

**Into The Dawn**

"Well tradition says that she was a prostitute and Jesus forgave her. She became one of His most devoted followers." I articulated.

Stephanie nodded her head.

I went on by asking her another question, "Have you ever heard of Rahab?"

Stephanie nodded.

"Well, she being within the genealogy of Jesus, one of His most distant relatives was a prostitute."

Stephanie looked at me with hope in her eyes.

I asked her, "Stephanie, could I pray for you?"

She replied, "Yes."

I got up and stood beside her, laid a hand on her shoulder, and began to pray for her. She immediately began to manifest a demon right there in McDonalds! Within half a minute I cast that demon right out of her with the authority of Jesus' name! No matter if it was a public place God was going to most definitely have His way to set Stephanie free that night! Later on we left that place feeling very encouraged due to what had just happened.

A couple of days later I had another divine appointment running into Stephanie once again outside of the Starbucks coffee shop. I asked her how she was doing. She told me that the devil was allowing her to listen to worship music but he wasn't going to let her to go to church. I told her that if she had Jesus that she need not fear the devil. I invited her to come to the Vineyard church whenever she was ready.

That night I interceded for Stephanie and prayed for Jesus to become her knight in shining armor and to rescue her from the grip Satan had on her.

Amazingly that Sunday she was in church lifting her hands in worship to our God. It was so good to see her liberated and enjoying God at church! Jesus is so noble and worthy as He answered my prayer in such a way to bring Stephanie home once again!

I heard that Stephanie went into a Christian women's recovery center, graduated, and then moved back to Ontario to be with her family. I consider that a success story and I feel very blessed to be used of God to help restore this girl. Stephanie, who was lost in the shadows of addiction and prostitution, had been restored and is now safely in the loving arms of the Father. That is a story of victory that I enjoy sharing with people from time to time.

**Into The Dawn**

## Chapter 31

One afternoon I called Roland in Kelowna from the mission. As we conversed I advised him that he should come to Kamloops and go into recovery with me. I explained to him that he would never be the father he is supposed to be if he keeps drinking and doing drugs. He agreed with me and told me he would think about it.

A couple of weeks later as I was on my way home from church my cell phone began to ring. I answered it and it was Roland. He told me that he was at the end of his rope and he was ready to come to Kamloops and go into recovery. He told me that he had received Jesus into his heart earlier.

I was ecstatic! He was now a Christian! I had been praying for him many years for that to happen!

Roland came to Kamloops on the bus and went into the men's shelter. This was a humbling experience for Roland as he had never been in a shelter before. We found out that the New Life Mission, where I was staying, wouldn't accept Roland because it is their policy not to accept family into the program. This was discouraging for us to learn, but I told Roland to have faith and that God was taking care of him.

A few days later I walked with Roland to the Phoenix Center detox where he was accepted. We prayed together before he went in and then I went home. After Roland spent a week in detox he was transferred to King Haven Treatment Center in Abbotsford. This was good because his son now lived in Abbotsford with his mom.

I was very happy when he told me one night on the phone that while in chapel he received the Baptism of the Holy Spirit. He finally understood what I was trying to tell him all those years when I was a Christian and he wasn't: God is real and He loves us! Now I had a true brother in the Lord and Zac, my nephew, had his dad back in his life!

**Into The Dawn**

## Chapter 32

The word of prophecy that I received from the Tuesday night church home group was constantly on my mind. God had revealed to me through them that He was calling me to minister to the First Nations people in this nation and beyond. I knew it was true but how could I acquire the passion that I needed to perform this task?

A few evenings after I was contemplating this I saw a story that came onto the evening News that sparked my attention. It was a story about a rash of suicides being committed by various First Nations youth in the northern region of BC.

The news cameras were filming a family who were casting the ashes of their recently deceased young family member off a bridge into the river below. As I viewed this sorrowful scene I perceived the distress of the mother who had just lost her son to suicide. She was crying tearfully with such anguish that it cut me right to the heart. I knew then and there that I had to do my part in order to help my people find God. They are hopeless and desperate without Him as we all are! The passion I needed to help God witness to the First Nations people was now fully ignited!

About a month later I received a prompt in my email that announced a Christian First Nations, National Forgiven Summit that would take place in Ottawa

Ontario. This summit, put on by Gathering Nations International, was in response to an apology made in Parliament by Prime Minister Harper. The apology was for the atrocities that took place toward First Nations children in the Catholic residential school system in times past.

The ministry, Gathering Nations International, began their "Journey of Freedom" in BC and ended it in Ottawa. They were going from one native community to another to rally survivors of the residential schools to come and attend the National Forgiven Summit in Ottawa. The message to the people was that forgiveness for past atrocities perpetrated towards them (by the priests and nuns at the schools) would bring them freedom from the spiritual maladies that unforgiveness and bitterness brings.

Like I mentioned, I really wanted to go to this First Nations summit in Ottawa but I didn't know how I would get subsidy for needed expenses. I decided to make it known to my Tuesday night home group details about the summit and that I wanted to go. One of the members pledged me $500 and when they took up an offering I received another $300. I was very excited as I now had the funding to travel!

I bought my plane ticket for a June 9 flight to Ottawa. My ticket would be cheaper if I would fly to Ottawa two days prior to the opening ceremonies of the Summit.

So on Wednesday June 9-2010, I caught an evening flight to Ottawa. I landed in Ottawa around 10pm EST and I departed the jet and made my way into the terminal. I planned on taking a taxi from the airport into town to the Jail Hostel where I would be spending two nights before I would make my way to the summit.

As I was moving down an escalader I noticed at the bottom a friend of mine from the home group in Kamloops. It was Lee! What was he doing here? I thought I was hallucinating!

"What are you doing here?" I asked him grinning ear to ear!

"I am visiting family. I am waiting for my daughter who is coming on a later flight." he answered with a big smile.

I told him why I was there and that I was taking a taxi into town to stay at the Jail Hostel. He shook his head and informed me that it would cost $40 to take a taxi into town. He told me that he, his brother, and daughter would give me a ride into Ottawa. Talk about a divine appointment! I had no idea it would cost me $40 to take a taxi and now I had a ride. This was unexpected but very welcome indeed.

So after Lee's daughter arrived they gave me a ride and dropped me off at the Jail Hostel. The Jail Hostel, located in the heart of Ottawa, is an old jail that closed in 1972. The purpose of the Hostel was to give tourists the chance to know what it was like to spend a night in jail. It cost me $35 a night and I was given a key. My cell was a closed in room, contained a thick black iron door, and the walls were made out of old red brick that added to the experience.

I spent the night and the next morning I decided that I would tour the Parliament buildings that were within walking distance from where I was staying. The Hostel was also located beside a mall so I went in and got a coffee from one of the baristas before I made my way up Wellington Street toward Parliament Hill. On the way I noticed that there were many large buildings that resembled castles with Victorian age architecture and had large flags flapping in the wind from the steeples displayed above. As I made my way up Wellington Street I came to the Rideau Canal. It was a man-made canal that connected Ottawa to Kingston on Lake Ontario. It was very beautiful and serene and I noticed that many people were using it for pleasure boating. I was also informed that in the winter it became the world's largest skating rink.

Ottawa was amazing, and everything I viewed was very interesting and enjoyable. Finally after a five minute walk up Wellington I arrived at the Parliament buildings. The architecture was remarkable. I decided to do a prayer walk around the buildings so that is what I did. After my prayer walk I went for a stroll along the Ottawa River that was below Parliament Hill. After my enjoyable walk I made my way to the Tomb of the Unknown Soldier. There were so many touristy things to do in Ottawa that didn't cost money.

**The Parliament Buildings**

**Eric Badke**

The Tomb of the Unknown Soldier

The Ottawa River

**Into The Dawn**

## Chapter 33

The next day I packed all my stuff into my packsack, handed in my key, and departed the hostel. I spent most of the day exploring Ottawa and when it came time to go to the Civic Center to attend the opening ceremony of the summit I caught a city bus and rode it with anticipation in my heart. I would be going to the summit by faith as I had no place to stay that night. It was too far from the hostel to make the commute every day.

Once I arrived at the Civic Center at 4:30 I went into the lobby to locate the information booth. Once I located the booth I approached them to inquire about a possible billet so I would have a place to stay after the opening ceremony. They told me that they would look into it and to return after the night concluded to inquire again.

I went in and found a seat at the top in the last row of the stadium seating arrangement. I noticed that there were only a few people there at 4:30 but at 4:55 five thousand First Nations people showed up at once. I said within myself that they probably decided to show up on "Indian" time!

This description of the opening ceremony is from int4canada.com:

*After five months of travelling across Canada the 'Journey of Freedom' the team led by Chief Kenny*

Blacksmith finally reached Ottawa for the 'National Forgiven Summit'. On a beautiful sunny evening, thousands gathered at the Civic Centre for an historic occasion where a coalition of First Nations, Métis & Inuit would, as individuals, respond with forgiveness to the Prime Minister's apology made exactly two years before to the day. On June 11th, 2008, Prime Minister Stephen Harper had sincerely apologized to the Aboriginal peoples and asked for their forgiveness for Canada's role in the Indian Residential Schools system. For many, now was the time to set Canada free through choosing to forgive and thereby gain their own freedom.

The arena had been transformed with vivid lighting and smoke effects and a wide stage had the outline of both a tepee and an inuksuk with a large screen between them. Chief Kenny Blacksmith opened with a big smile saying that we had waited a long time for this moment. He urged us to expect much from our Chief Cornerstone that weekend! Chief Kenny was partnered by Pastor Alain Caron from Gatineau who translated into French.

There was a very warm welcome from the local Algonquin Nation with a reading of Psalm 24 and a prayer that the 'King of Glory may come in'. Pastors Ken Hall and Ken Roth also welcomed the Summit on behalf of the Ottawa churches. Chief Kenny could now say, 'that we are free to do whatever needs to be done'!

**Into The Dawn**

*The nations came together to lead us in worship. An eleven piece, multi-ethnic band, that had never played together, excelled in leading us in celebration worship to the Lord. They started with, 'The Lord is gracious and compassionate ... ', His love and mercy being the basis of our being able to forgive others. Throughout the weekend the worship was vibrant and creative in song and dance. Many First Peoples dancers from across Canada combined with the drums, energetic and passionate, gave us an experience of Psalm 150 style worship. The Inuit throat singing was very special.*

*There were consecutive important addresses by Chief Elijah Harper and Chief Billy Diamond on Friday evening. Chief Elijah's vision was that the First Nations would be recognized in Canada as full equal partners and for them to live abundantly in their own country. While he was willing to express forgiveness to the Government he was also clearly looking for more apologies and more respect. He noted that the Prime Minister's apology was only for the Residential Schools issue and even that had been lacking in one aspect. He shared that at the time of the apology in the House of Commons, the Speaker actually left his chair and sat on the floor of the House, thus causing the Commons to officially become a 'Committee' instead of a full Parliament. Chief Elijah said that the Government missed an opportunity to treat the First Nations Leaders present in the chamber as equals and said that there was a lot of work to be done.*

*Chief Billy Diamond said that this conference meant freedom! At the age of seven he was torn from his*

**Eric Badke**

*parents and became a number – 316. His later joy was to know the power of John 3:16! In the church residential schools they had misrepresented the nature and love of God. They told him to pray to a God who never answered and he had felt abandoned and rejected by both his parents and by God. He shared that full healing came out of the divine order of repentance, forgiveness, reconciliation and restoration. When he heard the Prime Minister's apology he exclaimed, 'that the last veil of secrecy over Canada has been torn' He believed that the First Nations would bring revival to Canada and exhorted them not to stay in the prison house of unforgiveness.*

*Towards midnight David Mainse led a group of pastors in a Declaration of Repentance, kneeling before the aboriginal leaders and asking for forgiveness on behalf of the Church of Canada. In a very moving response Elijah Harper and Billy Diamond expressed their forgiveness.*

That night as I experienced the opening ceremony from the top of the Civic Center I noticed that there was a VIP seating arrangement on the floor below where chiefs, dancers, parliament members, and the media were sitting. I remembered thinking to myself that it would be an honor to sit down there among them.

Once the opening ceremony concluded it was about 12:30 am. I went out into the lobby and toward the information booth only to see that it was closed for the evening. Even though a slight panic swept through me, I decided that I would keep my faith in God that he would provide me a place to stay for the evening. I went outside to the front steps and watched as thousands of people walked by me, got in their vehicles, and left the scene. My faith was being stretched at that moment as all hope for me to gain lodgings for the night was diminished. I looked over at the lawn that was nearby and decided that perhaps that is where I would spend the night.

Within a couple of minutes a First Nations man at the top of the stairs caught my attention as he was bent over going through his packsack looking for something. I noticed an "All Access" pass hanging from his neck by a black string. Something made me go over to him and ask him if he was staff member of the event. He informed me that he wasn't. I then told him my situation and he asked me, "Oh you have no place to stay? Just wait here a minute."

He went down the stairs to an awaiting van to talk to a lady that was in the driver's seat. After a minute of them talking it over I heard her say, "He can stay with you."

The man walked back up the stairs and held out his hand. He introduced himself as Noel Pootlass and that he was a Hereditary Chief from Bella Coola, BC. I shook his hand, introduced myself, and told him that I was also from BC. He told me that I could stay with him and his three young daughters at a house that was nearby.

**Eric Badke**

**Chief Noel Pootlass**

Noel then asked me if I wouldn't mind going to an after-party first. I readily agreed so we got into the van and we drove to the Crown Plaza Hotel where the after-party was being held. I was excited! After we arrived we went up a private elevator to the Penthouse suite. When the elevator opened I noticed that the room was very classy. There were tables that held food and drink and tables in which to sit, converse, and eat. All the leaders from the Summit were there! After I had a snack with Noel and the girls I walked over to a large window that was arrayed from floor to ceiling that overlooked the city of Ottawa.

I pulled out my cell phone and made a long distance call to a friend in BC. I told her that thirty minutes prior I had no place to stay, that all hope was lost, and was planning to sleep on a lawn for the night. Now, due to the Lord providing with abundance, I had a place to stay for the weekend and was currently at an after-party where all the leaders such as: Kenny Blacksmith, Elijah Harper, Billy Diamond, and Linda Prince were. I told her that I had to hang up the phone because Noel was motioning me over to go meet Kenny Blacksmith!

I couldn't believe how blessed I was! When we got to the house where we were staying I was given my own room. It had its own bathroom with a Jacuzzi tub!

Noel and I talked late into the night and discovered that we had similar walks and beliefs.

The next morning after breakfast Noel gave me my own all access pass for the event! I now would have a floor seat near the stage along with all the VIP's of the summit! I couldn't believe it! We walked from the house to the arena and entered the floor area of the event. As I sat with Noel and his girls near the stage I felt honored to be among the First Nations, Metis, and Inuit leaders.

This description of the second day of the Summit is also from int4canada.com:

*The Saturday morning session opened with individual Inuit and the Métis also accepting the apology of the pastors. James Arreak said 'I choose to forgive you'! Pastor Eva Deer (Nunavik, QC) said 'Church of Canada, I forgive you; we are reconciled through Jesus Christ.' Métis Evelyn Lipke said, 'I also forgive and release you, O churches of Canada, from any judgments I have had'. A reading of psalm 126 also* summed up for Evelyn what she was sensing ...'when the Lord restored our fortunes ...'.

Chief Kenny explained that the Journey of Freedom had encouraged individuals to make a choice to come together and forgive. They were not speaking on behalf of anyone except themselves. Forgiveness was not political or economic, it was spiritual and it was for each person individually to make that choice. We then came to the time of Release. Chief Kenny read aloud the lengthy 'Charter of Forgiveness and Freedom' which declared forgiveness for many offences. 24 Elders who had survived the Residential Schools then signed the Charter on behalf of the coalition. This was then also signed by 12 young people with the hope of freedom for future generations, 'Let us break the yoke of the past, let us find wisdom and hope together'.

Opening the afternoon session was a spectacular Grand Entry of First Peoples in full regalia with feathers, furs and drums.

A most moving moment was when a dozen young children from the Flying Dust Reserve (SK) sang the National Anthem in Cree.

The Charter was then presented to the Minister for Indian and Northern Affairs, Chuck Strahl, who represented the Prime Minister. Due to international involvement Stephen Harper addressed the Summit by video affirming the Charter and expressing his support. In response Chief Kenny said 'Canada is a healed Nation, more healed today than before because of *what we were able to sign this morning. Mr. Prime Minister, we forgive you!'*

*Chief Herman Yellow Old Woman then pronounced that Chief Kenny Blacksmith and Chuck Stahl would be given the highest expression of honor to recognize those who want to do more. In an elaborate ritual with a buffalo dance, ancient songs and impartation, they were given the right to wear an impressive headdress. 'This would make them stronger leaders'. Other gifts were given for the Prime Minister including a handmade paddle for the healing journey for Canada. Chief Noel Pootlass (Bella Coola, Nuxalk), anointed Chuck and Kenny with eagle down and the fine filaments were carried out over the congregation for peace and blessings. This was now the time to embrace and celebrate freedom. Jonathan Maracle then led us into loud celebration with his Native Mohawk Fusion Band.*

This is a description of the final day of the Summit:

*Sunday continued in celebration and included an extended ceremony of appreciation, honor and highest respect for David Demian and his family. He was presented with a variety of gifts and it was declared that David's walk and influence through Watchmen for the Nations had been an indispensible factor in bringing the First Nations leaders into unity. His example of allowing the Spirit to set the agenda in the Gatherings had become the model for their present and ongoing journey.*

**Eric Badke**

Inuit throat singers

The Charter of Forgiveness

**Into The Dawn**

Chief Herman Yellow Old Woman

Eric with "All Access" Pass

**Eric Badke**

When it was time to go home Monday morning the woman who generously let Noels family and I stay at her house paid the $40 for my taxi back to the airport. What favor from the Lord! I had so much to be thankful for as I experienced my culture come together at this Summit and forgive. After the "Charter of Forgiveness and Freedom" was presented into Parliament Saturday afternoon there was a release in the Spirit that could be felt by all those in attendance. After that, the summit turned into one big celebration as there was dancing, singing and drumming being enjoyed by all. I will never forget it as I also found my dance while attending this summit.

The next evening, after I returned home from Ottawa, I attended the Tuesday night home group. I had a praise report for them and they were anxious to hear it. I explained to them in detail all the events that took place at the summit and they were very uplifted and encouraged. A month later I announced to the group that I was leaving Kamloops as the Lord was now leading me to Abbotsford to be near my brother. They prayed for me, spoke to me words of knowledge, and sent me on my way.

## Chapter 34

After spending ten months at The New Life Mission in Kamloops I moved into a third stage recovery house in Abbotsford BC. I lived there for four months and then moved to another recovery house called Joshua House. I spent the winter there and in the spring I wanted to get involved in First Nations ministry.

I contacted North American Indigenous Ministry (NAIM) and asked them how I could serve. They informed me about a summer ministry program that they held every summer in Saskatchewan. They had a three week option and a seven week option. I was very interested in attending the three week option but I was once again faced with the issue: how would I get the money to go?

At the time I was attending a church men's group and I told them my intentions to attend this Summer Ministry Initiative (SMI) in Saskatchewan. A very good friend of mine also attended these meetings, and he offered to pay for me to go. Late June I received permission from the executive director of Joshua house to attend this ministry initiative.

After I concluded the NAIM Summer Ministry Initiative (SMI) I was asked to write a summary of my experience in Saskatchewan so they could submit it into the NAIM newsletter-Fall 2011 issue. After a lot of work this is what was submitted:

**Eric Badke**

*A Summer Missionary's Experience…Greetings, friends. My name is Eric Badke and I am half Okanagan/Salish First Nations (on mother's side) and half German (on father's side). I am 39 years old and live in Abbotsford, BC. I have a desire in my heart to see God move in the First Nations communities. I knew the Summer Ministry Initiative would give me a taste of what First Nations ministry is like. I also knew it would be a life transforming experience!*

*Brian Fink, SMI Director in Saskatchewan, put me in touch with another SMI'er from Washington State: a Vietnam vet named Joe Shepherd. He came up from Washington, picked me up in Abbotsford, and gave me a ride to the orientation. What favor! Joe and I became great friends as we embarked on our journey east, sharing with each other our testimonies!*

*Starting in late June, we had an amazing 25 days in Saskatchewan. First we received some training. We worked with NAIM staff, Brian Fink and family, Neal and Darcy Alsbach, Tim Bryce, and Clyde Cowan, who is NAIM's Executive Director. The four-day orientation was amazing as we fellowshipped, laughed, and learned about evangelizing the First Nations.*

*They placed Joe and me on a team together, and our assignment was the Fishing Lake Reserve eleven kilometers (seven miles) outside of Wadena, SK. We met NAIM missionaries, Mike and Gloria Gunnon, and stayed with them the first night. They brought us to the reserve the next day and introduced us to the Chief of the reserve. The Chief's brother graciously offered us* his home for the coming weeks. While attending a community Canada Day event the first evening we found that the residents of Fishing Lake were strong in character, genuine, and kind towards each other and us.

We weren't too sure how to approach the residents of Fishing Lake, but the following morning God inspired us. We came up with three events that we were to present to the reserve: a week long program called, Spirit of Truth Week! The Gunnon's joined us on this endeavor. We created and handed out 130 flyers, one to each house, and received a warm response.

Spirit of Truth Week resulted in mostly kids attending. We held a movie night, teen night, and a five day kids club. The kids were precious; and twenty to thirty came at a time. We offered Christian based activity: Scripture memorization, prizes, instruction, games, and snacks. We all had so much fun!

Teen night was also a success with twenty to thirty teens attending. I remember as we were having hot dogs around the fire one of the teen girls asked, "When are you going to teach us about God?" That was music to our ears! We prayed with the teens and then Mike Gunnon spoke about Christ and what it means to become one of His followers. We also had the opportunity to answer questions as we drove some of them home after.

I believe we planted some seeds for the Gunnon's to water. Joe summarized later, "there was fertile soil with

**Eric Badke**

*the teens at Fishing Lake reserve." Please join us as we pray that many at Fishing Lake be awakened and come to the revelation of God's saving grace, Amen!*

*After three weeks, Joe and I said our goodbyes at the reserve and headed to Fort Qu'Appelle for the SMI Recap. After Recap we were sad to leave but we have many new friends, photos, and fond memories.*

*Thank you Father God and NAIM for this opportunity. It was a blessing and a growing experience for all of us. I strongly endorse this ministry, and encourage anyone who is available to come out next summer and discover how wonderful this program really is. I guarantee it will transform your life! So until next year – K'iche Manitou we embrace you! Brother in Christ, Eric Badke*

**Teen night**

**Into The Dawn**

**Kids club**

It was a pleasure attending this program. As we were leaving Fort Qu'Appelle I went over in my mind the events of the past three weeks I spent at Fishing Lake reserve. There were conversions to Christianity while we were there but I worried about those who converted. I was concerned that the seed of salvation that was planted within their hearts might be choked out by the cares of the reserve.

I thought to myself wouldn't it be nice if there was a residential cultural "Discipleship Center" in which new First Nations converts could leave the cares of the reserve behind and come to this center, dwell, and be discipled for a lengthy period of time? They could build a foundation in the word and learn the spiritual disciplines in order to become disciplers themselves. Afterwards they could be sent out into the mission's field and it would perhaps turn into a movement that would spread across the nation of Canada like a wildfire and eventually go to the nations of the world! Feedback from all over the world shows that First Nations people have a high credibility as missionaries;

because people know their history, their pain, and they highly respect them.

**Into The Dawn**

# Chapter 35

It was also during the orientation at SMI that I was befriended and invited by Tim Bryce of NAIM to go to Baja California, Mexico for three months beginning on February 18, 2012. I was very excited at this idea to go to Mexico and volunteer at Foundation for His Ministry, Home for Kids Orphanage. I was told that I would also have an opportunity to go on outreaches to the surrounding communities to evangelize the Triki First Nations that resided down there.

I spent months fundraising and I also received my passport. Finally in February the day came when I would leave to catch my flight from Bellingham, Washington to Los Angeles, California. In LA I would meet up with a NAIM Youth group who were also going to the Orphanage. I would get a ride and spend the first week with them at the orphanage.

Once I boarded the jet in Bellingham we took off and flew into the sky. The G-force on take-off pressed me back into my seat which is always a unique experience. It wasn't long before we were above the clouds to where it was sunny. The clouds below me looked like white, fluffy cotton balls. I ordered a Pepsi from the cart and listened to some music during the flight. I caught a nap and woke up at 5:30 just in time to watch the sun go down. The magenta hue of the sunset was mind-blowing as the sky above it turned a dark shade of blue which to me looked very majestic and royal. The first stars began to poke through the curtain of night. Before long I was able to view the lights from the city of LA. What an astonishing sight as we flew lower and lower on approach to LAX.

I could see lit up subdivisions, eight lane highways full of commuters going here and there, and main streets spread out as far as the eye can see. As I focused my eyes I also began to observe palm trees lining up in the center of the streets and I was thrilled to see them! I had never laid eyes on a palm tree before.

Finally we landed and I expected that after I got off the jet it would be California hot but it was actually jacket weather. Anyways it was nice to finally arrive at LAX. I had never been to LA before.

Once in the terminal I made the long walk to the baggage claim where I would meet up with Joe Lopez. Joe is an Apache Native American who is affiliated with NAIM. He volunteered to pick me up and take me to the church where Neil and Brian's NAIM youth group was staying for the night.

So we collected my bags and hopped onto an airport shuttle bus which brought us to where Joe was parked. After we got into his truck Joe decided to show me the ocean, so we drove near Santa Monica. It was nice to see the beach at night with the four foot waves crashing in. The atmosphere was balmy and it was neat to be in LA with all the palm trees and the California architecture in the houses.

**Into The Dawn**

After the beach we went to "In N Out Burger" and it was a good to experience a restaurant that is native to the States. The burger that I ordered was delicious!

After the restaurant we went to the church. No one was there. We waited for two hours then went for a drive. When we got back we noticed that the two vans had arrived. It turned out the reason for the delay was that they went to Costco and got lost in LA coming back to the church. It was nice to see Brian and Neal again. I hadn't seen them since the Summer Ministry Initiative in Saskatchewan.

Most of the group was already bedded down for the night but I got to meet a few young men from the youth group: Martin who is a guitar player/enthusiast, Shawn who they called "Chief", Carl and Samoa Brian. We socialized for a bit and then went to bed. We were all excited that we were going to drive to Mexico the next day! It was enough anticipation to blow one's mind I'd say!

The next morning we woke up nice and early and drove down the street to a breakfast diner. Most of the group walked down earlier and I was surprised to see how many from the group were at the restaurant; there were about eighteen in all.

I ordered bacon, eggs, hash browns, toast, and coffee. After breakfast we went back to the church and packed up the trailer that was connected to Neal's van and then we hit the road. I was given the front seat in Brian's van. I was very tired so I took the opportunity to

**Eric Badke**

catch a nap. As we traveled south I would wake up every fifteen minutes or so and look out at the scenery. It looked like I was in dinosaur land with the trees the way they were.

Finally I woke up for good when Brian said, "There's Mexico!" In the distance you could see a very wide hill with a multitude of houses on it. That was Tijuana! We stopped in the border town to get gas, vehicle insurance, and use the facilities. We then drove to the border crossing and for the first time I saw Mexican Federals with assault rifles. Both vans got searched and then we were approved to drive into Mexico.

I had been waiting for this for over six months and finally I was there! I could tell I was in Mexico because the land was teeming with poverty, broken down houses, and graffiti. At the same time, as we drove along the ocean the scenery was breathtaking and the houses were charming down near the beach. Some of them weren't complete and I saw a few large hotels that were half built and had been abandoned for years. As we journeyed down the peninsula of Baja, California, Mexico it was nice to see the ocean, palm trees, and the coast as it was a pleasant hot sunny day.

On the way there were Mexican Army check points and the men had machine guns like they did back at the border. Neal's trailer was searched again much to our amusement.

**Into The Dawn**

As we toured, everything I looked at was thought provoking and interesting because to me everything I saw was brand new. When we arrived in the coastal city of Ensenada, 125 km (78 miles) south of the border, we saw a lot of tourist attractions from the van. Periodically the smell of seasoned steak from the taco stands would waft into the van through the open windows to fill our nostrils with a gratifying aroma.

I was taking a lot of photos along the way mostly of the palm trees aligning all the streets and looking very prestigious. It was wonderful to be surrounded by Mexican culture. We could hear Mexican music coming from El Comino's at stop lights and from large speakers set up outside of the taco stands. Eventually we were through Ensenada and into the mountains. The highway was treacherous at times as it was one lane each way. We saw at least one accident along the way.

About three hours later we arrived at our town of Vicente Guerrero. At the only stop light in town we turned left and began the final stretch approximately one mile down a dirt road toward the Mission. The first building we came to that was on the property was the Mission Church which was quite large. Across from the church was what looked like a very long two story motel. That was the Bible school. After we passed by the church and the school we could see that about a quarter mile down was the orphanage on the right side of the road. We pulled into the visitor's center on the left. We were finally at the end of our journey.

**Eric Badke**

For over six months I had imagined what the orphanage would look like and this wasn't anything close to what I had imagined. It wasn't one large building like I thought but many one level buildings that were connected together. There were flower gardens and palm trees everywhere

We were met by a Tim and Debbie Bryce of NAIM and local named Uriel. Uriel, our host, told us where our rooms were in the visitor's center. Neal requested that I have my own room because my snoring kept him up the previous night in LA. So Uriel said I could move into a room on the second level of the visitors Center. I took my bags up to my room and then laid down for a rest.

**Visitor's Center on the Left**

**A Sunset View from the Visitor's Center**

**A Prayer before Outreach**

Eric Badke

Before long Neal knocked on my door and informed me that it was time to head over for evening church. It was 5:45 pm. We walked as a group the five minute walk to the church and there were already a lot of cars in the parking lot. When we entered the church there was quite a few locals there and it was lively. The band up front on the stage played an upbeat song and people were clapping, singing, and testifying! There was also a row of young women up front below the stage with tambourines that had tassels hanging from them. They were performing a routine to the music hyping up the parishioners. It was fun to watch as we stood as a group up in the balcony and clapped to the beat of the music. This church was definitely alive with passion for the Lord! We were also given translation devices with earphones like they have at the UN in New York City so we could have the message in English as the pastor spoke in Spanish. That evening the pastor spoke a great message about not sinning.

The next morning we went to Sala (daily morning church from 8-9am) and then we went on a guided tour of the property. It is large! The property includes a visitor's center, a gift shop, an internet hut, a gymnasium, and seven houses for orphans ranging from babies to teens, a large dining room, a free daycare for working moms in the community, a prayer garden, a soup kitchen, a dental and medical clinic, a warehouse, a custom wheelchair shop, and a macadamia nut processing plant. The processing plant was affectionately known as "The Nut House".

**Into The Dawn**

We were told on the tour that when the orphanage first started out they had an experimental garden to see what would grow on the property. They found out that Macadamia nut trees had the ability to grow there which is an unusual occurrence. Usually Macadamia trees only grow in Hawaii and Australia. They decided to grow one hundred trees but then they went through a frost and then went through a drought. Eighty trees died and it upset the director of the orphanage. The head gardener told the director not to be upset but to rejoice because now they had twenty drought and frost resistant trees they could graft off of to make more. The Lord has a habit of bringing the good out of the seemingly bad.

Now the foundation has an orchard with frost and drought resistant macadamia nut trees-about two thousand in all. There are also orange, lemon, grapefruit, and guava trees in the orchard. Most who have experienced it would agree that there is nothing like tasting a fresh orange or grapefruit picked directly from a tree!

The rest of the week consisted of child evangelism, outreach to the migrant camps, and work in the orchard, garden, kitchen, and sorting macadamia nuts at the nut house. We had such a good time and I must say the First Nations youth from Saskatchewan were strong in character and very funny. On Friday afternoon we had the opportunity to go to the park just down the road to an outdoor market, there was so much for sale and I bought beautifully designed woven friendship bracelets ($1 each), a nice red and white woven poncho for 150 pesos ($12).

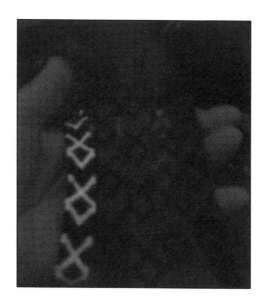

**Friendship Bracelets**

**Me in my New Poncho**

**Into The Dawn**

On Saturday we went as a group to the beach. It was a beautiful sunny day and it was exciting to witness the vastness of the Pacific Ocean in its splendor. Some went fishing and others collected shells. After searching among the rocks and tide pools for about forty five minutes I found an amazing conch shell. It was a keepsake that I would bring home with me after my stay in Mexico. It was too cold to swim although a few brave souls went in and body surfed the waves. There was also a young girl from our group who got baptized after being a Christian for a year and that was special!

So the next morning we sadly said our goodbyes. The youth group headed for LA to go to Disneyland and then drive the long road home back to Saskatchewan.

**Sunset at the Beach**

**Eric Badke**

# Chapter 36

At the Mission new church groups would come in from the States every Sunday evening (45 in all) and they would usually leave the following Saturday. Since I was staying for three months I was now considered a staff member at the orphanage. I worked at the nut house (drying, cracking, sizing and sorting macadamia nuts) and I went on evangelism outreaches to the surrounding community five times a week. I loved every moment that I was there especially interacting with the children. Rededicating my life back to the Lord twenty-nine months previous to my arrival at the orphanage was the best decision I ever made!! It brought me to an amazing place to fulfill my God given desire to perform His ministry.

Here are some journal entries from Wednesday March 6 and Thursday March 7, 2012. This is just to provide insight into how life was at Foundation for His Ministries (FFHM).

*Wednesday March 6*

*This morning I woke up at 5:30 am like I have been for the past two Wednesdays. I had coffee and then met Tim at his van. We then picked up Richard who is the interpreter. He had another coffee for me which was an added blessing. We then drove thirty minutes to the Rancho de Christo Rehab Center for morning devotionals. Rancho de Christo is a rehab that is connected with the Mission. After the men complete the program they have an option to go to the Mission's bible school if they can acquire the funding to go.*

*It is so peaceful and quiet at the ranch as the property overlooks the ocean. The Lord is very much present with the men there. When we entered the building where morning meetings were held we shook hands with the men (ten in all) then they stood and began with a song in Spanish and clapped their hands. These men are so adorable and have substance as do most Mexican people. After a prayer Tim led the men in a devotional and Richard interpreted into Spanish. It was very insightful and I knew the men really appreciated having us there. I will be sharing my testimony and a small teaching about character building next Wednesday at the ranch.*

*So we drove back and arrived in time for 8:00 am Sala and then at 9:00 I went to work sizing Macadamia nuts at the nut house.*

*At 2:00 I met with Eleanor (An elderly Caucasian lady who has been living at the mission for 20 years - she is cool). We went out in her car (my third time) into the community for outreach to the Triki First Nations who came from Oaxaca (Southern Mexico) to harvest fruits and vegetables. It was an extraordinary privilege to go from one makeshift house to another meeting with kids and parents. I would practice my Spanish on them and give them gum. They seemed to like the gum and the smiles. I also brought balloons for the kids; I would blow them up, tie them off, and give it to the kids to bat around. It is just nice for them to have someone who cares come to visit and we try our best to reflect the light of the Lord into their lives. I feel for those people but I know by how Eleanor responds to them that as time moves on, living conditions are getting better for* them; an answer to her prayers. The Lord is taking care of them amen. One thing I do notice is that a lot of these makeshift homes have satellite dishes on the roofs and the parents always make sure their kids have clean clothes even though they don't have a washer or dryer. They use a scrub board and a clothes line which does the trick.

So that evening I went to Wednesday evening church service with Tim. It was very lively and enjoyable as usual and that concluded the day. Thank you Lord for your provision and grace.

Thursday March 7

I went to Sala at 8:00am and then sized nuts in the morning. At lunch Ureal (one of the hosts) gave me the keys to #9 my new small trailer. I was impressed!! It has a nice yard with a deck, flowers, cactuses, and a five foot palm tree. Inside is a living room with a couch and easy chair, a table that can seat four comfortably, a kitchenette, a small but effective bathroom with a shower, and a cool bedroom in the back with a queen sized bed. Nice!! It also has skylights that open up and all the lights and outlets work!! The doctor who just left the Mission used to live there so it is stylish. The Lord had me in mind for this trailer and it just so happens that my favorite number is nine.

So at 4:30 Tim and I joined the visitors for outreach to the migrant community and I am so happy that we went!! We drove four church vans about an hour south and when we arrived in the community we parked in an open area, set up a loud speaker, and cranked the festive Christian Mexican music. When the kids showed up the party started!! We joined them in throwing balls, Frisbees, skipping rope and I was giving out gum like crazy! Later we gave out Christian coloring books and new packs of crayons and soon most of the kids knew that I was the main hook up for that and I made sure all new-comers got some.

When it got dark we showed a Jesus film (projected onto the side of a van) in Spanish and there was about three hundred people watching including us from the foundation. After the film a prominent Spanish speaker from our group spoke of salvation on the microphone and afterwards did an alter call. All came forward to receive Christ through faith and prayer! God drew them in and it was so encouraging to witness that!! Afterward we gave everyone a New Testament Bible in Spanish.

I noticed earlier that a car pulled up during the film and they stayed in the car and listened with their windows open. The Lord prompted me to go over to that car and I gave the man in the driver's seat a Bible. He turned on the interior light in his car so he could glance at it. I taught myself a little Spanish earlier so I said to him "Ola, Nuevo Testamento!! Jesu-Cristo est Salvador. Espiritu Santo en corazon-Hermoso-para siempre" which when translated means "Hello-New Testament-Jesus Christ is Savior. Holy Spirit in the heart-beautiful-forever"

The man, I noticed, had alcohol on his breath but I could tell he was impacted by the Spirit and perhaps looking for a better way. I pray that the Lord would show him and his family a better way through the *infilling of the Spirit and the revelation through the word amen!! The Lord was generous this night as the moon above shone full and bright and the stars twinkled and winked. Everyone went home with a fire ignited in their heart and a new hope on the horizon.*

*So we departed and when we got back to Gurerro we went to "Smokies" an outdoor taco stand for grilled steak mozza cheese tacos with lettuce and hot sauce - so sublime!!*

*What a great couple of days and I have another five weeks to go :) During a prayer and fasting event last Friday the host said, "There are three types of missionaries: those who go; those who give; and those who pray." Father God please bless richly all those who have contributed for me to come here and also prayed for this to happen. The Lord planted me, watered me and I believe He has brought me to this place to bloom and I want to do what is right.*

In all I had an amazing three months in Baja California, Mexico. The last three weeks, while Pastor Tim went north to the States, he gave me access to his jeep which was handy. I had two good friends at the Mission: Josiah and Jonas. We would have fun taking the jeep out into the desert and up into the mountains.

**Into The Dawn**

# Chapter 37

When my three months were up I said my good byes and my friend Richard drove me to San Diego, California. Once in San Diego I caught a flight to Bellingham, Washington. I had someone pick me up from Bellingham and bring me across the Canadian border into Abbotsford.

I spent the next couple of months planning for my next mission's trip. I would once again join up with NAIM to attend Summer Ministry Initiative in Saskatchewan. This time I chose to attend the seven week option. After the orientation I was put on a team with two twenty year old men named Sam and Bryson. We were assigned to a small town in proximity to eleven reserves in northern Saskatchewan. The name of the town is La Ronge. Here are a few journal entries from my time in La Ronge:

*July 8, 2012*

*Well, it is day eight of NAIM's Summer Ministry Initiative (SMI) and it has been quite an adventure thus far. It is so beautiful in Saskatchewan where we are (La Ronge) but there are a lot of horse flies and the mosquitoes come out once the sun goes down.*

*We are staying with a family here (NAIM missionaries- the Clarks) and my team (Three of us: Bryson, Sam And I) are staying in tents out in the yard.*

*On Friday we went out on the lake in a motor boat to go fishing for Northern Pikes (Jacks). It was so very beautiful on the lake and there was also a rainbow. I* caught the first fish right away and after about three hours we had about eight fish. When we arrived back at the house that evening we had a nice outdoor cook out - deep fried Jack in batter-very nice!

We have also gone to the beach three times and there is an eagle that flies over the lake every time we swim there. Today the horse flies were swarming around me and I was bitten today about fifteen times! They chased us all the way home! Nasty little critters!

Anyways, we are having a discouraging time when it comes to our witness in the community. There are so many reserves here-eleven in all. There are many houses and this is not a place of destitution. Most people here have money as it is one of the richest reserves in Canada. Most of the time people come to the Lord when they are out of options, but these people have plenty of options which make's a conversion to Christianity almost impossible. The Native band also owns a gold mine just north of here.

Ben Clark who is a NAIM missionary stationed here says that there is no point trying to reach adults or elders in the area because they don't listen. He says that the best thing to do is to reach the kids and then they in turn will reach their parents. We have looked at the summer schedule for the area and there are many sporting events that we can attend. We just have to find stuff to do for the next six weeks.

Anyways, we are blessed to be staying here with the Clark family as they are very nice and easy to talk to.

**Into The Dawn**

When Jesus was in ministry he was so busy that His disciples could hardly keep up. Jesus only did what the father showed him to do. I am praying for the Father to show us also what we need to do in La Ronge this summer.

July 27, 2012

On Thursday we went to Redmen's (he lives about 20 km in the bush) and put up some poles, twelve in all, for Elliot's (Ben Clarks son) dog sled team. There was an insane amount of horseflies out there swarming and circling all around us. Yesterday we picked up the dogs and brought them out to Redmen's, hooked them up, fed & watered them.

Last night at about 7pm all of us guys Ben, Elliot, Sam, Bryson and I went out to Potato Lake to go boat fishing. Even though we didn't catch anything it was fun and for the most part: therapeutic. I needed that. When we arrived home we played the board game "Risk" and that was also entertaining: full day.

Today (Saturday) I slept in until 12:30 and after I had a shower we went out and did some work taking down and rolling up chain-link fencing for Elliot's puppies. We will put it up on Monday. That will also be a full day.

At about 4pm Sam, Bryson & I walked to the Co-op grocery store and it took us fifty minutes in the hot sun. I am glad there was a breeze along the highway. When we arrived at the Co-op we purchased cold drinks and I needed to get a $10 Telus long distance prepaid card. We then walked into La Ronge and it is very nice downtown. The main street travels along the edge of the lake and we can see floater planes taking off and landing in the lake periodically. The summer setting in this Saskatchewan town was very picturesque; the big blue sky with the billowy white clouds all arrayed in its splendor declaring the Lords majesty!

I was able to minister to eight people on the way home and glory to God it was such a privilege to be an ambassador for the Lord! The first man we encountered we met on the street. Sam and Bryson walked to the beach/park while I talked with this man. He was slightly intoxicated. He told me that he was a strong believer in the Lord but he was having problems with alcohol and heroin. I was able to share with Him how the Lord set me free from addiction and with his permission I was also able to lay hands on him and pray. I got his Facebook information and I am going to help him go into recovery. His name is Henry John Macleod and he is First Nations.

So we did a fist bump, parted ways; and I walked on to where Sam & Bryson were waiting for me at the beach/park. We sat at a table, had a rest, enjoyed the summer breeze, and said some prayers. When we were on our way out we encountered three First

Nations men who were sitting on a bench drinking vodka and tonic. They were very friendly, they introduced themselves, and we talked to them for a while. I told them that I had three years of clean time and they seemed surprised by that notion. One of the men asked for $5 and I told them that we had something better than money: Christianity! Then I noticed that one of the men's front pocket was hanging out and was empty. I said to him, "I have something for your pocket!" And I slipped a "Steps to peace with God" Bible tract into his pocket and he said, "Oh, thank you." The man who was sitting next to him, who was deaf, pointed to his heart and then to the sky indicating that he also was a believer. He readily accepted a Bible tract. After we concluded our conversation we said our goodbyes. The man who didn't accept a Bible tract mocked us but it was nice to be an ambassador for Christ all the same.

So we continued our journey home and by the time we reached the end of the main street the pavement turned into gravel. We were on the Little Rock reserve (one reserve among the eleven in the area); our short cut home. There was some nice shade from the trees on the side of the road, thank God; and a breeze, amen.

By the time we were on the other side of the reserve and near the highway, we came upon a house where there were four First Nations, two men and two women, sitting on the front steps of their house. They called me over. Sam & Bryson walked on. One of the men wanted to know if I wanted to smoke a marijuana joint with them and I said, "No thanks, I am three years clean." And he said, "Wow! How do you do that?" I told him that I couldn't have done it on my own but I had help from a higher power. The other man asked me if I was a Christian and I said, "Yes." He told me that he tried Christianity when he was a kid but it wasn't a "good fit". Then he said, "But I am glad that you have chosen the path of righteousness."

He philosophized for a while and then I asked him if I could give him some reading material and he said, "No you cannot." I asked him, "Are you sure?" and I pulled out a tract. Then the man who first asked me if I wanted to get high with them said, "I'll take one." That made me happy that he was interested. I pray that the Lord will continue to strive with him and the others. I ended our divine appointment by saying: "All I know is that my life has become more abundant since I have chosen the path of Jesus." and the man who accepted the tract said, "We all have a purpose." and I replied, "Amen!" I bid them farewell and I walked on.

Sam & Bryson were waiting for me sitting on a large rock near the highway. I joined my brothers and about fifteen minutes later we were finally home. We had barbeque burgers waiting for us. Thank you Lord for the witnessing opportunities this day in La Ronge Sask. I feel very encouraged and perhaps a few seeds were planted today. It may be that we can meet again to water those seeds and the Lord can provide the increase in His timing.

August 15, 2012

My team and I just spent ten days at our host's cabin five hours south of the Northwest Territories. It was very remote and very beautiful with lots of fir trees and lakes. You can drink out of any lake up there and the water is just like store bought! We went out in motor boats, caught plenty of fish (including a 20 pound trout), shot and butchered a moose, roasted wieners and had smores around the campfire at night! With God's grace I was also asked to preach last Sunday *morning and since there were two non-Christians present I spoke on John 4. If you drink the water that Jesus offers you will never thirst again! I also had my own lake (south-side) with my tent by it but it is good to be back at home base in La Ronge - hot water, power and internet so nice - His mercy!*

So it wasn't very easy spending seven weeks in La Ronge. Most of the time I was out of my comfort zone, but it was an experience that I will never forget. I am so thankful I was given the opportunity to learn that not all missions' trips are easy but can be quite challenging. I faced many tests while in La Ronge but at least our team made a small impact while ministering there.

I did end up going back to Baja California, Mexico for two weeks in February and two weeks in October 2013. I absolutely loved going there for the second and third time! I am so thankful for my friend who provided most of the funding for me to go!

**Eric Badke**

# Chapter 38

In February 2014 I moved into the Samaritan Inn recovery house as I still struggled with pain medication. The house can receive ten clients who have a burning desire to overcome addiction. The facilitator's names are Paul McKee and Tom Wood. Every day we received instruction from the word of God. Tom and Paul are using scripture to help build up our character so that we can be more like Christ. We were building a foundation on the Rock (not sinking sand) so that when storms of turmoil come we are not easily blown over and destroyed. I spent six months at the Samaritan Inn and then in September 2014 I moved to Vancouver to attend First Nations Bible College (FNBC).

FNBC is a free Bible College and is a two year program. It is located right in the heart of East Vancouver (Main and Hastings). I found a room in which to dwell right around the corner from the school so that was beneficial. The school itself is three days a week: Tuesday, Thursday, and Friday 11am-2pm. We would study a different Biblical subject every week and have plenty of reading homework. We also had a test every Friday afternoon. Every week that was completed equaled one credit and one needs forty credits to receive a Four Square pastor's certificate.

The school was being held at Street Church and our instructor, Randy Barnetson, is also the pastor of the church. Street Church has three services a week: Sunday, Wednesday, and Friday evenings. The church would give away six hundred hot dogs a week, two hundred per night, to the street people who would line up to receive.

So I attended the first year of college, made a lot of friends, and also had the opportunity to volunteer at the church preparing and giving out hot dogs. I also volunteered with Salvation Army's "Food on the Corner" program three evenings a week.

In February seven of us from the Bible College went on a mission's trip to northern BC. While we were up there we went through Kitwanga where I spent many years as a kid. It was nice to return there once again and see the place where I used to live. This is an email that I sent to my friends summarizing the mission's trip to northern BC:

*Greetings in the Name of the Lord! Just a quick update to let you know that the First Nations Bible School Just completed an eight day tour of northern BC. It was an amazing experience!! We ministered at six different Native churches in Kitimat, Terrace, Gitanyow, Gitsegukla, Kispiox, and Nazco. It was a blessing to perform songs, share our testimonies and we each took turns preaching. After each evening concluded I felt so full of the Holy Spirits love for our hosts and the people we ministered to. It was amazing!! I had an opportunity to preach in Gitanyow. I also performed a song called "River of Life" by Jonathan Maracle of Broken Walls on the native drum which was a privilege. I am so happy - I just discovered that I can do that!! Well that is just a quick update and God bless!*

**Eric Badke**

**Eric Preaching in Gitanyow**

**Northern Missions Trip**

**Performing at Church**

**Into The Dawn**

# Chapter 39

While in Vancouver I also met a man at a Church leaders luncheon named Ron who I shared my testimony with. He was impressed with what I told him and he advised me to write down a mini testimony so it could fit on two sides of one paper. He would then print out one hundred copies and we would give them out on the street in the hopes that my testimony would draw people into God's Kingdom. I decided to take on this project and it took me six weeks to refine it down and complete it. They were printed out and we began to give them out on the street. I hope that people were influenced by my "life story" to the point where they would decide to convert to Christianity like I did.

As this book is coming to an end I have just one more thing to add: I want to let you know that if you are lost in the darkness like I was, Jesus came as a light into the world so that those who believe in Him shall not abide in darkness but have the light of life. God is inviting you to become a member of his family. Jesus died on the cross for our sins and was resurrected from the dead for our justification on the third day. How you respond to that is on which your eternity hangs. With Jesus as your savior you can have a full assurance of an eternal Heaven after passing on from this life.

I used to be a child of the night but when Jesus came into my life I entered "**Into the Dawn**" and became a child of the day. Since then I have never been the same and I now have a flame of hope burning within my heart. I want that for you as well.

**Eric Badke**

I will never know until I get to heaven how my "life story" made an impact on the Vancouver city streets. I decided that I would end this book with it:

My Life Story - Eric (Sept 2014)

My name is Eric. I am 42 years old, born in Kelowna to an Okanagan/Salish First Nations Mom and a German Dad.

Looking back on my life of hardship and peril, I now realize that Jesus was always there upholding me through every storm.

When I entered my teens I began to rebel and my Dad would punish me by locking me in my room and beating me with his fists. It was a hopeless situation that seemingly had no end. I wanted to get back at him by becoming a criminal, so I began breaking into other people's homes. Eventually when I was seventeen I was busted for B&E and was sentenced to twelve months open custody.

It was hard doing time in juvenile prison because there were many gang members there who had a desire to prove themselves. After being beat up on a regular basis I began to fight back. When I was released from jail I came out worse than when I went in. I moved to Hope BC and became a drug dealer. I became popular and I encouraged all my new friends to be as much of a menace to society as I was. It was us against society, I was a bad example, and proud of it!

The Bible says in the book of Proverbs that, "There is a way that seems right unto man, but its end is the way of death." As I continued my life chasing meaningless pursuits to make money I was never satisfied. My mind became drug addled and I began to feel like a walking gutter. What I didn't know at the time was that there was a God sized void in my heart I was desperately trying to fill with drugs, alcohol, and money! The party life was weighing me down and I desperately sought reprieve from the depths of spiritual despair.

I was a walking shell-that is until one night in my room I had an encounter with the Living Jesus! I realized in my awoken spirit that my life up to then had become meaningless. I became very much aware of my sin and I decided to make things right with God. I felt the most intense love coming into my room and I felt His unearthly forgiveness and peace! It was that moment that changed it all! God became real to me for the first time in my life and He filled that void in my heart that I was always trying to fill with other things that could never satisfy!

I had just had heaven open over my life, God became real to me! I thought to myself, "I've got to take some time off and figure out what

**Eric Badke**

this means!" Eventually I came to believe that God wants every individual to experience the same "life change" that I went through. He wants to capture one hundred percent of your heart as He captured mine and gave me a purpose in life!

First Nations people have always had a heart for their own people. It wasn't long after my conversion experience that God placed within me a desire for First Nations ministry! I soon joined up with North American Indigenous Ministry (NAIM) and became a missionary to a couple of reservations in Saskatchewan two summers in a row. It was a life transforming experience learning just how genuine and kind the natives were in Saskatchewan. The Spirit of God told me that His First Nations People are "precious lively stones" to Him made beautiful through much trials, hardships, and testing's. These are "fires" that the Lord knows well! He has a special plan for His First Peoples in North America!

Learning the Bible and being in full time ministry has also brought me to the mission's field in Baja California, Mexico to create a bond with the Triki First Nations. It was another amazing life transforming experience as I made so many new friends, learned a little Spanish, and got to experience life in another culture. I also volunteered my time going on many outreaches to the surrounding communities. I was well received and I found the people there to be strong in character and caring toward me and each other. As another ministry opportunity presented itself I also attended the First Nations National Forgiven Summit in Ottawa. It was remarkable and I feel very optimistic that as you decide to put the Lord first He will bring you the same kind of experiences one day!!

Now as summer 2014 comes to an end, The Lord has brought me to Vancouver to attend First Nations Bible College at Street Church. I feel called to represent The Lord in the downtown area and volunteer my time. Since Jesus captured my heart it gives me pleasure to bring God to those who desperately need Him.

I have a genuine concern for you my friend. I want you to know that Jesus loves you and wants you to experience His faith, hope, peace, and life abundant. According to Jeremiah 29:11 He has plans for you, to prosper you and not to harm you, to give you a future and a hope! God loves to shower beauty on the ugliest of circumstances. Look what He has done for me! I encourage you to draw near to God and His great Holy Spirit will strengthen you and guide you into all truth.

The eagle was made to rule the skies my friend! I urge you to surrender yourself to become that eagle of strength & power Jesus wants you to be! As you call upon the Lord His Spirit will cause you to mount up and soar on wings as eagles to rise above the clouds of affliction, oppression and addiction. Remember: He desires to transform your heart and provide you with a fulfilling and abundant life! Choosing to trust Him will quench your "spiritual thirst" and guide you to a place of wonder and excitement as He has guided me! I just have a desire in my heart to leave you with this Bible scripture that means the world to me. Thank you for reading my life story-God bless you :)

*I waited patiently for the Lord, and He inclined to me, and heard my cry. He also brought me out of the horrible pit, out of the miry clay, and set my feet upon a rock, and gave me a firm place to stand. He has put a new song in my mouth, a hymn of praise to our God...many will see and put their trust in Him. (Psalm 40:1-3)*

Manufactured by Amazon.com
Columbia, SC
30 March 2017